Blue Garden

Blue Garden

Witold Poplawski

iUniverse, Inc.
New York   Bloomington

iUniverse books may be ordered through booksellers or by contacting:

iUniverse
1663 Liberty Drive
Bloomington, IN 47403
www.iuniverse.com
1-800-Authors (1-800-288-4677)

ISBN: 978-1-4401-7276-2 (sc)
ISBN: 978-1-4401-7274-8 (dj)
ISBN: 978-1-4401-7275-5 (ebook)

Library of Congress Control Number: 2009937475

Printed in the United States of America

iUniverse rev. date: 10/26/2009

To those who care about children in danger or dire need.

For my wife

Contents

Part III : Garden of Shade

Part IV : Mediterranean Gardens

Foreword

Often life unravels very differently than we would expect. We are given opportunities to examine our heartbreaks and our gifts. Surprisingly, sometimes our heartbreaks reveal our greatest gifts. Perhaps the key is to be open and go inside ourselves.

The journey into self-discovery is the longest and deepest journey of all. With poetry and prose, Witold illuminates and gives us guideposts on this journey. The twists and the turns of lives lived and lives still evolving are captured for our reflection.

This fascinating work is in a style that is simple yet complex. Laying down creative thoughts in poetry followed by an innovative prose reiteration puts the poetry in motion. The result is delightful. The gardens of light and shade in concert with the subsequent Mediterranean gardens take us deeper into understanding the human spirit, as well as the brilliant mind and courage of Witold Poplawski. He has given us stories to ponder in glimpses of his background and family, all woven into a descriptive manual for living. There is a driving force of goodness—it is in us all—and when we embrace the positive in our fellow man, we become fully human and fully alive.

Eugenia and Anna must be delighted—you will be introduced to them later in the book.

There is much food for thought in this work. While it has been said, "It is comforting to know that whatever happens tomorrow will have absolutely no effect on today," how we think today *will* define all of our tomorrows.

Let's open the door to the blue garden.

—Grace King, author

I Am Listening

By Grace King

I am listening for the sound of her breathing, the shallow assurances of the fact she is still alive.

I am watching the closed door in front of me to her bedroom. I am afraid of what might be laying on the other side. I want to reach out and turn the knob, but I hesitate, I am frightened. I am frozen and silent. I want the courage to turn the knob. I want the courage to be able to face what may await me on the other side.

How many mornings have I experienced this? How many times have I walked this fine slender edge, this surreal experience? It is difficult to attempt to put into words the living agony of this fear. Most will never experience this horror, and I am grateful, for no one would want to experience this.

I listen, I almost stop breathing trying to quiet my body, trying to tune my ear to the sound, any sound of life beyond the closed door. How long can I stand here? How long can I keep the silence of the pain that is screaming inside of me? How still can I be? How long must I endure this agony?

How long, gently and slowly I extend my right hand and grasp the cold knob of the door.
What will I do if she isn't breathing? What will I do if she is as cold as this piece of metal in my hand? How will I hold on to my lifeless child? How will I face this when it finally comes?

Gently, I turn the knob and slowly the door opens.

Author's Note and Acknowledgements

This book is a charitable project. It stems from my belief that in tough economic times we ought to offer more support and charity to others in dire need, to break the adversity, while reaching out in friendship as we do so. My proceeds from the former project, *Inner Voice* (Tate Publishing, 2008), assisted "street kids" via Covenant House, an effective charity in Toronto. Similarly, my entire proceeds from this volume go to the reputable and very efficient Leprosy Mission Canada, also in Toronto, for helping to cure leprosy in children. Leprosy is curable; the medication, priced at a dollar a day, has to be taken for one year. Their families cannot afford it. When you buy this book, you provide medication to a child with leprosy for about one week—and hopefully have a memorable read! Each time fifty-two books are sold, a child is cured, restoring normal life to that child. Yes, it could be as simple as that.

I wish to gratefully acknowledge Anna Hutchinson for her invaluable contribution and Grace King for her inspiring and helpful comments, as well as to thank my editors. Grace took care of her special-needs child for many challenging years. She has graciously agreed to include her poem, "I Am Listening," into the foreword of *Blue Garden*.

Introduction

Perhaps an artist's ideal expression would be to create a cohesive work in more than one form, appealing to the full spectrum of all five senses. Think of a literary text accompanied by music composed for it, further strengthened by visual images—perhaps a series of relevant paintings, even sculpture—all accomplished by ... one artist. Some artists have reached towards this ideal. For example, nineteenth-century Lithuanian artist Mikolajus Curlionis painted cycles of pictures centering on profound themes and composed symphonies to "illustrate" his paintings. English poet William Blake and Lebanese philosopher Khalil Gibran both illustrated their mystical poetry with their own paintings. American Albert Du Aime exhibited his paintings under his real name and wrote books inspired by them under the pen name William Wharton.

Unfortunately, my ability for this prolific artistic display has been nil. In *Blue Garden*, however, I have inched towards it by using two different, consecutively presented, literary forms. I call this method *hyb-writing*. My aim is to assist in fusing cognitive and emotional connections within the "innermost" perception of the reader through both disciplined "clarity poetry" as well as focused stories, varied as human life might be. If poetry identifies, condenses, and defines a chosen theme, prose exemplifies and expands upon it. Life itself—being the best writer—offers us its gifts in brief moments of poetry and longer periods of daily prose. In the same vein, this work aims to tune into the natural rhythm and melody of the intricacies of human life.

It is my hope that this method will foster in the reader a more reflective, in-depth relationship to the topics I'm exploring. Thus, hyb-writing results in *hyb-reading*.

Blue Garden gets its name from the view the astronauts had of planet Earth from dark space. They saw a strikingly lonely, beautiful "blue garden." The book is composed of four interconnected parts. The first, "Garden of Silence," reflects on the specific, subtle shades of everlasting meaning that permeates silence. This part consists of fourteen poems, all relating to one prose piece. The next two parts, "Garden of Light" and "Garden of Shade," strive to explore human virtues and then our vices. Using the method of hyb-writing, each of the twenty-four poems is followed by a short, corresponding prose companion. Some of these diverse stories are based on factual events, others are mostly fiction, some even science-fiction. The fourth part, "Mediterranean Gardens," touches on concepts of beauty and joy, hailing the creative powers of the great unknown. These concepts are expressed through poetry and, as in the first part, include a single prose form related to them.

Part I

Garden of Silence

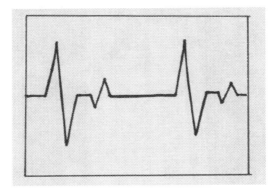

The first and the simplest emotion which we discover in the human mind, is Curiosity.

—Edmund Burke

Till Our Awakening

Are there silent mystery-bytes, in which this world
Curiously appears to breathe outside
Its plainly coexisting with us daily-ordinary?

Via those elusive bytes, floating beyond known,
The chance to touch that extraordinary in our lives
Can hum and flee like a tiny bird, ghostly-swift

A heart may sense such a calm moment unforeseen
When a flock of graceful cranes
Flows over a red half-shield, in their loud wavy stream

Someone's mind may ponder it deeply
At the museum in Siena, as feeling halted by a picture
With a quiet power, or the face of Christ

A group of pilgrims might experience such a byte
On a vibrant carpet, while praying
With their heads bowing towards far Mecca behind dust

A port town beggar could, suddenly, feel touched by it
If he looks in the eyes of a stranger
Who just offered him the warmly bighearted in alms

All these stealth, precious wonder-bytes
Like the rosary's beads connected by a living thread
Sum up, counted by invisible fingers till our awakening ...

The Three Eagles

Vast powers of the first eagle appear unmatchable,
As it carefully brings in its mighty claws
The undefined mystery
Or us,
To the hard-nest universe's part by destiny found

Here—the still indeterminate riddle
Or us,
Evolves into a multifarious process defining itself
As a human life on Earth,
Which the eagle exited quietly
Having made sure a life it had brought could hatch

The much elusive second eagle
That hovers deep within sunlight over our lifespan
Out of the finest-in-blue descends at times
And in its shiny claws
It carries the most precious gift—the enigma of love

This sacred eagle makes sure that life, like a chain,
Continues with itself,
And its experiences of falling in love
Gradually model for the state of loving all what is

Finally, the third eagle silently descends
To firmly take
The by now exhausted but still unresolved mystery,
Or us,
Inserting it with care beyond the density dimension
Into the snug nestle of light

Is the third baffling eagle the same as the first one?
Is it identical with the second?
Does its threefold glide define ash-worthy Phoenix?

The Most Silent Voice

Born sceptics among us
In human narrow senses trust
And avoid that voice
For them, it does not exist

Most of us barely hear it
As it eludes our ears
Via alleged vast distance
Thus we reach out
Towards wise intermediaries
Or good translators
Placed in-between a listener
And the voice "afar"

As all humane characters
We, listeners, respect
Our own parents
(Fading into the azure soon)
So tend to follow
Such intermediaries
And these translators
Our fathers and mothers
Inherited thus adhered to

The noble risk now posed is
That a keen listener,
May in-trust mistake
The words of feeble humans
For that original
First and last voice,
Impossible to mimic,
The hardest to interpret

Why do exist some
Yearning to sense its silence
Feel what it does not say
Could merely ears heed it?

Acceptance

—For my son

Without first accepting myself
Could I ever
Accept another?
I ought to start
Erecting the foundation
Of self-acceptance

However,
How could I in truth
Accept myself
If I would not
Acknowledge the pristine, silent flame
Lit within
This thin glass lamp
Of my bodily existence?

In full surrender
To the ocean of silky-soft flames
Feeding all life
From within,
May we await the gifts
Left on the path to acceptance

Empathy

A life calls for commanding well the two parallel languages:
Audible, of words, and silent, of feelings

They strive to overlap, while remaining distinctly different,
With both being indispensable
For steering safely through the social narrow straits

To simply define thoughts via uttering of all the proper words
Likely would not be enough
To fully communicate with anyone intelligent and sentient

That person would readily expect the silent parallel translation
To the wordless language of feelings,
Through the fine affective transmitter, understood as empathy

Empathy relies on the truest, falsification-proof, innate ability
To foresee and graciously calibrate
One's own emotional impact on all the others one relates to

It also most naturally tunes to other people's in-depth feelings,
Its twofold magic signalling to them
That one is emotionally safe to talk to, and warmly interact with

Luckily for the empathy-shy, even a seemingly foreign language
Could be learned if one sincerely desires to explore it ...

Compassion

—For Grace King

Within a soft net of warmly pulsating infinity,
Compassion may signify *the force*
That asks hurting self-conscious existence
To soar towards the utterly healing zenith

If the universe's exhausted matter
Vanishes in wonder behind the black holes
May compassion's light arrive
Through mirror "holes" in colour white?

To see the fearless compassion incarnated
Feels like sensing in disbelief
An on-target, arrow-like messenger
From beyond the too obvious obviousness

The quiet power commanding altruism alive
May have inexplicably originated
In the mysterious *source* of compassion

Had *it* bestowed through betrayed sheer love
That innermost living letter,
Sealed on the Mount of Sermon
Sent from the dark-moon mount of lone cross?

Sound Bytes from Silence

—In memory of the children who vanished during the Holocaust.

Softly, surrounded by a fringe of inquisitive bright creatures, itself a silver shape beneath the steadfast constellations, Simon's dead body moved out towards the open sea.
                                   —William Golding, *Lord of the Flies*

It all started when his widowed mother, a refugee from the destroyed Polish capital, Warsaw, brought five-year-old Victor to a compact apartment in a large, old, grey building they moved into. It stood in the historic, medieval city of Krakow.

"Who lived here before?" asked the boy, never having seen anything so old before.

His mother, even though she always tried to be cheerful talking to Victor, answered with an unusually sad expression, "On this street, before the war, lived Jews only."

What was this? Intrigued, Victor persisted, "Who were the Jews? Were they like us? Could you show me one?"

His mother hugged him. "Some people have done awful things to them," she said simply, "so the Jews are not around anymore." Considering all that had happened in Nazi-occupied Poland and elsewhere, she decided perhaps her answer had been too understated. How would her son feel about her if she tried to protect him from the truth? She added, "I can't show a Jew to you. They all got killed."

"Who killed them and why?" Victor insisted.

"You are too little to understand such things. Some very, very bad people did this to the Jews," said his mother. "You ask so many questions. But it is time to go to bed now."

Startled, Victor had difficulties falling asleep. His boyish mind tried to picture the Jews living here before, in this very room, in this very spot where his bed was placed now. What did they look like and what were they doing? Were any children here? What would it be like to talk and play with Jewish children? He wanted to ask more questions about those mysterious Jews, who vanished from this street, adorned with tall acacia trees that each spring displayed their small, resilient leaves. So little did he know ... How many exterminated victims similarly vanished from the many old streets like this on the European continent?

9

Victor's questions, nevertheless, brought him little information. He grasped only that something inexplicably horrible had happened to all Jews. He eventually found pictures in an old book of Orthodox Jews, in what he saw as "old-fashioned" black clothes and white socks. *So that's what they looked like*, he thought.

After a few years, the little boy had friends on that quiet street. He spent long hours with them, playing soccer with other boys and doing what boys do. But they weren't his life. He needed to pursue his own, very different interests. Quite often, he could be found walking alone along the narrow and neglected, grey streets. He would enter the open doors of dilapidated buildings and pass through dark halls to melancholic yards. Yards he knew the Jewish families used to utilize. He would sit there, thinking. He could feel a mystery here, almost hanging in the air. Even the faint sunbeams penetrating the crowns of old trees took on a different quality here.

Victor was puzzled by the alphabet on some of the old shop signs painted on walls as grey as the street. Hebrew. Some were in Polish too. Victor could read those. Like the one promoting "Hats! The City's Best!" with a painted black, round hat peeling off a wall overlooking the ancient Jewish cemetery of "Kirkut." Just two minutes' walk from Victor's apartment building, this mostly abandoned cemetery slept close to the medieval synagogue Remuh. Victor felt compelled to climb its brick wall and explore what was hidden behind it. He walked beside the graves, built so different from the Catholic graves he'd seen, with some stones already collapsed, others bent under the weight of time.

He came across a very old grave and stopped before it. Rabbi Isserles. It struck him for reasons he could not fathom. It would be years before he learned about this famous leader. Then he would think back on this day and remember all of it. Much later, his written for the ordinary people hence published in a local newspaper poem, Victor's literary debut, reflected on that cemetery.

The Old Kirkut (Cemetery)

A shy spring pauses at the muted plots of nostalgia in green,
Within which by someone's deft fingers
And attentive eyes forlorn
Have survived in-stone encrypted verses in Hebrew
Hiding under moss,
Where at still, as if crystal nights,
By gentle wind touched new fluid gown of a weeping willow

Whispers eulogies in Yiddish
To an aging wall slowly bending forward,
Or bowing in its brick's silence
To Rabbi Isserles's near-abandoned grave
Yet over that silence had passed the blindest and blade-cruel
From all hurricanes possible
That has sent the thorn-eclipsed children
Of the entire vibrant House of Israel
To their heaven's synagogue
One so vast that endless
Where—in welcome—invisibly have stretched
The glowing with love candleholder's seven silver arms ...
Faithfully following its too long absent owner
A round black hat, painted above the forever closed shop,
Also had stealthily flown away
Leaving behind on the peeling wall, only the faint shadow
Protected by a fading sign,
Written in the evenly encoded, and ever puzzling alphabet

Victor's precocious quest to learn more about the Jews was too slowly unfolding the enigma of their massive disappearance. He started asking the adults in his life more specific questions. One evening, he heard a story about Jews whose lives his father had saved though he had not even known them. Victor asked his mother whether she had also saved any Jews. His ill mother, though frail and only a couple of years from her early death, recounted one experience.

"There was a little boy who had apparently escaped from the Warsaw ghetto. One day, he knocked on my door ..."

"What happened next, Mom?" Victor asked.

"He was hungry. I gave him as much food as he could pack. I gave him everything. Everything I had.

"Even your own food?"

Victor's mother looked down, remembering her own hunger.

"But, Mom, couldn't you take him in?"

"You don't understand," she said most sadly. "For taking that boy in, all of our family could have been killed on the spot by the Nazi occupiers. That was their law in Poland, strictly enforced. And then you would never have been born ..." She smiled, then added, serious again, "Even giving him food could have brought the same fate, according to that inhuman law. But after looking in that boy's eyes ... I took the risk."

For a long time, Victor thought about that boy from the ghetto and his extreme distress. How would it be to escape from that death-sealed ghetto? He tried to picture himself in such a dire situation. How would he feel, walking hungry along the forbidding streets, in desperation knocking on unknown people's doors? All the time knowing that he would be killed if caught, merely because he was … whom he was. That perspective was extremely bleak and frightening. He could not fathom why certain people were so incredibly cruel to Jews. Why didn't all the joint armies of the world's soldiers defend them sooner? Why did no one come in time? He felt proud of his father's defiance of the inhuman Nazi law. How many like him were there? He later learned that quite many were, if not enough.

Soon Victor had to deal with other problems than the predicament of that anonymous Jewish boy. His new dilemma was incomparably milder than that boy's, yet challenging enough. His long ailing mother passed away. Then his grandfather. There was no one to take care of Victor anymore. He had to take his fate into his own hands. For the time being, the sad theme of Jewish annihilation, strangely puzzling and profoundly touching him, would retreat into the back burner of his mind.

Now, if any society could be compared to a barrel, Victor found himself at the bottom of it. He was just a poverty-stricken orphan, the lowest socioeconomic layer in an enduringly poor postwar country. Mercifully, he did not fully understand the scope of his miserable social pit. Victor just carried on with the life he'd been given, doing his naive, but sincere, best to fend for himself. In his eyes, his parent-protected school friends lived on the moon. Practical Victor did not waste time envying them. Rather, he accepted that this was the way things were for him. His peers might have a grievance with their parents grounding them for a day or two. He might have a problem arranging his next meal. When one of his friends complained, with tears in his eyes that the bicycle his dad bought him was too heavy and old-fashioned, Victor listened, all the while calculating in his mind how many buckets of coal he would have to carry to how many floors in order to buy a pair of shoes for the approaching winter. So he worked like a dog, getting ever stronger, and learning fast about life in his reality.

Adolescent Victor's life was certainly not monastic. He had a social life as righteously immature as any of his friends'. The older ones helped him make the most out of mistakes any unsupervised teenager could make. Despite all odds, he stayed in school. But a clipped-wing formal education was not where his mind dwelt. His circumstances required clear focus on objectives, to be met by effective actions. They were also urging him to activate any dormant potential, or else. The intensity of that effort and a necessity-bred creativity pushed his thinking to the extreme. He was honing his abilities to deal with his problems—be they physical or intellectual—with action, and in his own way.

The main physical problem was that, despite his best efforts to be prudent and hardworking, Victor went to bed hungry sometimes. But instead of asking for handouts, he decided to exert extra physical effort, even while hungry, and break through the obstacle. He took his inspiration from a thin handbook featuring a young American soldier, Steve Reeves, one of the pioneers of bodybuilding. Fighting the Pacific War, Steve exercised with heavy-guns' ammo. *If Reeves*, thought Victor, *better fed, but shot at, could train, I—worse nourished, but not shot at—can train.* He made his own equipment, filling different-sized cans with cement mortar, connected by scrap-metal pipes he found and cut to an appropriate length. He lifted these weights at home, particularly when hungry. On such scarce days, cold water from the tap would suffice; it could fill his stomach all right.

The gradually emerging physical and psychological results showed him that he was right in his defiant approach to adversities. They were there to be prevailed upon, period. After all, he was still very poor, but increasingly muscular and self-confident now. His uncompromising approach towards overcoming given obstacles caused a few raised eyebrows among those whose lives were shaped more smoothly and conveniently. Victor learned to never be concerned with raised eyebrows, unless they belonged to someone he had a very good reason to respect.

Being more physically competitive, Victor secured better odd jobs. Any physical obstacle was a breeze compared with other challenges in front of him. It become more important to Victor to satisfy his need to grasp as much truth as his mind could extract from the world around him, and extend it far into the universe. Not astronomy, not physics, but a universe that was emotionally close to Victor: philosophy, the nature of being, the center of the universe where all things began and ended. Where he could feel his own essence looking back at him.

The best way to approach that elusive truth was to see what the most profound minds had discovered, prospecting it over the ages. While just getting by in school, Victor embarked on a strenuous study of the world's thinkers, beginning with the available texts translated from Sanskrit, like Rigveda. A destitute teenager with no money to buy books, he trawled the municipal libraries. Then he discovered the many university libraries and sought them out. Krakow was a highly intellectual, artistic city as it turned out. He began to learn how the various creators of philosophical systems, of main religious theorems, and some genial writers in particular, had perceived us human beings, so recently, so temporarily, situated in this part of the endlessly baffling universe. Sometimes a strange feeling came over him like he understood something truly deep within himself. Most of the information felt foreign, however. He would need more time to digest it, cognitively and emotionally. His initial conclusion was that the truth he pursued must be incredibly complex. Even these learned minds were unable to fully grasp it. Despite the solitary night readings, the focused and intense thinking, he was not even close to understanding the nature of reality and the human condition.

Subsequently, Victor decided to examine not only the information, but also the motivation behind those thinkers' search. Did they ponder these universal truths only for themselves, for others, or both? Or, was it yet for some other reason? What made them address this growing tree of life? Surely, its roots were hidden and being fed from elsewhere. And what about that baffling *elsewhere*—what was it, where was it, *why* was it? He realized if one were to develop a greater understanding, one first had to work on oneself. He understood it would take much more time. Perhaps he should start with more readily available details, the *here and now*, and tackle the omnipotent general down the road.

There remained around him much to discover and analyze. Thus, he embarked on figuring out what mechanisms operate behind the surface of the society, day to day, be it politics, wealth, or religion. He soon discovered the major obstacle to such theoretical studies: the lack of distance to the studied subject, including his own lack of the self-distance, not allowing one to perceive one's own motivation and actions more clearly.

Victor felt that his own emotions were colouring his perceptions, protecting him through some wishful thinking, from seeing reality as it is, whether frightening or just plain ugly. He feared that self-protectiveness extended to his self-perception. It might be clouding his recognition of mistakes he'd made and weaknesses in his character. Accordingly, he wanted to eradicate that protection and improve himself, strengthening his heart and mind to observe the world with as much clarity as possible. Working on it, even without knowing it, he was already dismantling his defence mechanisms bit by bit, seeing them as a psychologically harmful "immune-system of the ego," parallel but in contrast to the invaluable physical one. Eventually he became able to very normally and calmly ponder the themes that others instinctively strayed from, to readily feel good about themselves, and so soothingly linear, rewardingly uncomplicated surface-world around them.

Although Victor gained a degree of distance to himself, what about the distance to the very subject of his quest? His original aim was to attain the best possible perception of truth, in and behind everything available to his observation. Soon he discovered, however, that his perception had been, like one of everybody else's he knew, entirely dependent on the concept of time … More precisely, it was totally anchored in his particular time of his lifetime. All people appeared to be referring everything to times they directly perceived in their short lifetimes. They were invariably living mentally in the unchallenged grips of their time. Could one arrange for some mental liberation from that tight grip, to gain more distance, despite existing just in this very lifetime? After some self- training, like often placing himself mentally in different times and eras, Victor, still being a tiny bird fleetingly sitting on a given-to-him thin branch, ceased to feel hypnotized by the perennial snake of time. He did not constantly look in its never-changing eyes, while being snowed by a confusing flurry of apparent "changes." Rather, he looked into those shapeless eyes when he preferred, except for the required practical, mundane duties.

This approach had some benefits regarding his quest. For instance, it was easier to figure out the real origin and flow of world affairs. Now, he could more easily discern true statements from deceit. He could see the past in the present. How the movers and shakers of today made the same statements, took the same actions, and had the same motivations as those belonging to others like them decades or ages ago. Now, he was free to understand their support systems, power ploys, their potential for good or ill, and their needs in the present better. He was trying to zoom in on what was going to happen. The future unfolded in his mind sometimes like colourful kaleidoscopic sequences. At other times, it was as if through the eye of a microbiologist, as he observed the constantly changing, fluid shapes of possible things to come under the microscope. The past, the present, and the future became all one, an ever-evolving multidimensional image.

He could see it in the continuous alteration of the borders of civilizations, their transient status from ruler to ruled, their growth and stagnation, their expansion, shrinkage, and collapse. He could see it in the continents' outlines themselves, with their infrequent but spectacular changes. He could see it in fashion—the bizarre evolution of societal dress codes coming full circle from the uncomplicated clothing of ancient times to the elaborate peacock periods to the increasingly simplified, almost uniformed clothing of the future. Perhaps, after all, time was itself a non-existent *snake?* Maybe it just amounted to the speculative milestones people were erecting as regularly as they could, to mark the perceivable changes in the material realm temporarily surrounding them …

For example, while talking to a vital, grown man at the newsstand, he pictured him as a toddler, a boy, as a young man, and then as a somewhat tired middle-aged man, an even more exhausted retiree, and then to the essence of the man at the moment of his death or the moment of his conception. What is the same in all those incarnations of the same being? What is different? What constitutes the enigma of life?

Victor moved his self-training a step further. Now, talking to the woman at his neighbourhood grocery shop, he pictured the bioelectric impulses constantly firing in her nervous system, the sheer miracle of her fragile skeleton, and the protective, elaborate sculpture of the skull. There seemed to radiate a flame of subtle energy surrounding her heart, evolving to other flames—flowers of energy. He did not literally see those pictures, but somehow they were quite vividly reflected in his mind.

As odd as these exercises seemed, Victor started to feel how profound and precious, delicate and complex, unique and beautiful any human being is. They helped him begin developing what later in his life would become a general love of human beings, although not of some of their feelings, thoughts, and behaviours. Victor did not really know why he was making these efforts to perceive the essence of things, the atomic and quantum realities, to see others as they intrinsically were, to understand the mechanisms of the world as it actually operated, in his perception. He did not fully understand yet what a high emotional price these efforts would cost him, or what an exhilarating journey it would be towards the light beyond.

In the tangible world, though, Victor did not have any particular problems with meeting his everyday needs. His intellectual search and physical labours were progressing on par with each other, as if he was quite harmoniously living and operating in the two seemingly separate worlds. But he did not talk to his school friends about any of his own, unfolding developments in either world.

An obligatory bus excursion sponsored by his school, brought him face to face with his earliest questions about the world: the enigma of Jewish annihilation. By now, he was older, well-read, and knew the main facts of the Holocaust. What he knew did not prepare him for what he saw in the place called Auschwitz. This Nazi SS–operated concentration camp was only some fifty minutes drive from Krakow. The visit shook him to his core. In the bus on the way back, Victor could not join the conversations of his schoolmates, who didn't talk about Auschwitz. He sat in silence. His own difficulties and obstacles went to oblivion, pathetically ludicrous compared with what he saw and sensed.

It was not just the huge dusty piles of eyeglasses, shoes, and suitcases exposed behind the glass. It was not even the thicket of artificial limbs surrounding them. More than these, it was the silent anthem of suffering he could hear playing non-stop behind the iron-blade gate. It sang beneath the stern ribs of the red-brick buildings. It clustered around the vivisected spine of steel rails where the crowded trains stopped to make way for the death-selections. It rattled in the hellish red-brick skull of the crematorium. Victor knew he would have to return there, but alone. He felt compelled to absorb the memories of voices he heard in the clamour. And try to understand the meaning coded in their soundless anthem.

After saving enough money for the trip, Victor returned to Auschwitz for a second time. Now alone and on his own time, he again went to the heaps of earthly belongings of the murdered human beings, predominantly Jews. He made an effort to picture in his mind the frightened eyes, still alive behind those dim glasses; the warm, sweaty hands unnecessarily hauling those once stuffed suitcases, and the sore feet that trudged to their executions in the now bone-dry shoes. It wasn't enough. He knew he had to look from behind those eyes, walk in those shoes, and hang onto one of those suitcases as if it mattered. At least for a few steps. He took a deep breath and closed his eyes, just as he had done in his mental exercises before. He could not. There were too many of them; he was too young; his mind was too weak; and his heart yet too closed. Overwhelmed by these mute artefacts of unimaginable suffering, he slowly walked along the dim corridors hung with grey photographs of the vanquished victims and survivors. He traced their paths among the grim, forbidding buildings mostly undisturbed. Visitors in those days were few and far between.

Eclipsing the barracks, rusty, electric barbed wires extended from perimeter to perimeter along rows of broad concrete poles. Victor came to the stark building that housed the crematorium, set somewhat aside. He went in. Looking at the dark metal doors to the open ovens, Victor hoped to reach back in time for just a moment and imagined himself sending support and compassion to the souls who had burned here. His thoughts felt weak, his attempts ineffective. He could not reach them. Perhaps the very walls surrounding him, formidable and deep as they were, bounced his thoughts back, repelling his good intentions. He left the crematorium, unsure how to proceed. Emotionally drained, Victor decided to return home.

However, a quiet voice within him told him to go where there would be no tourists. After a long walk, he entered the actual heart of the Auschwitz concentration camp system: Birkenau, with its endless rows of forlorn barracks. There was no gate, no guard; perhaps they had been completely forgotten. There was no problem getting in. The fence was broken down and in some places non-existent; a few of the barracks had lost their doors and some timber. Still, they all appeared to be intact.

Victor was hit by an aura of absolute abandonment and the utmost melancholy. How strange to feel the wind gently blowing in the crisp, autumn air. Like an eternal end of seasons, in the silence of a forsaken island, his own steps the only sound disturbing some vague presence that lingered beyond his senses. He did not know whether it was a welcoming presence or not. His inner voice told him to pay respect to it. He stopped, and in the humblest way he could, asked that presence—maybe it was just the wind— for permission to be there and to help him learn. He sat down in the high, uncut grass, eating a slice of bread and drinking water from a glass bottle. He received no answer.

After a short rest, Victor went through a number of barracks, examining them from the inside. Rows of bunks and dingy, worse-than-spartan, "bathroom" areas bordered on the surreal. A small chunk of grey petrified soap. Torn scraps of a crude blanket. He couldn't stop thinking about the people who attempted to warm themselves with these blankets in the middle of the winter. Or to wash their fading bodies with grey lather under frosty water. The infinitely morose place held him there with its sad force and eventually he realized he'd missed the bus back to Krakow.

He had no money for a hotel, but here was a free roof over his head, he thought. Under the circumstances Victor decided to stay the night in these Birkenau barracks. As it grew dark, Victor felt the silence around him expand into that darkness. He lay on the hard, cramped bunk and felt a sudden extraordinary feeling of loneliness overpowering him. It threatened to engulf him in all the darkness of this cruellest of worlds. He tried to remember how his fate differed from the fate of those who had occupied this bunk before: *I will leave this place tomorrow;* he reminded himself. *They could only exit through the chimneys of the crematorium converted into billowing smoke.*

Now, Victor could do what he could not do in the daylight. He began, quietly at first, putting his feet in the shoes of the tormented human being who slept on these boards until he perished. He could nearly hear his night's solace coming in silent prayers to Adonai. The humbling faith of an anonymous and forgotten man rang through him.

The silence itself changed around Victor in his half-sleep state. It appeared to be imbued with *clusters of emotional meaning* floating in it. If the air can murmur, whisper, cry, or pray, such sound-bytes were permeating into a cryptic, solemn melody. The teenager listened, first with his ears, then with his heart. It was as if someone or something—or some things in a multitude—reached towards him from somewhere else, trying to express itself. Victor wished his mind were not so weak and that these mysterious sound-bytes from silence would come in words much clearer, their meanings less garbled, and from a universe much nearer. Yet, as he drifted into sleep, deep within his heart, "the true him" delicately and inexplicably touched the subtle shades of a complex, beautiful, and most tragic meaning as they spoke—or sang—to him in no language he could identify:

"You have come here compelled to pause on the material steps of the invisible monument to human suffering," said the murmurs in the barracks at Birkenau. "This monument, the highest on the planet Earth, reaches above the clouds, vanishing beyond the stratosphere. We are the ones who built this monument with millions of imperceptible, yet blood-red, phantom-bricks. Each brick is made of an essence of individual human martyrdom, and they all comprise the abysmal epitome of the collective, *matchless human sacrifice*.

"You do not belong here, but we allow you to stay, as you came sincerely, to try to understand the bottomless abyss with your naive, if open, mind. What we convey, only an open heart can absorb and understand ... That is why we let you stay—to listen to our monumental silence. Like matter is built of atoms, this silence is comprised of sound *bytes*. These are the thoughts and feelings, particularly the feelings, of once-living entities. The sound bytes left by those who suffered are the strongest ... and last the longest. Ours has been the most tragic symphony of human suffering ever written or expressed ...

"We are the sons and daughters, many of us little boys and girls, of the ancient, long homeless tribe. We have been, most literally, the chosen ones. A fraction of us have been chosen to excel creatively and brilliantly in areas of importance to humanity, be it science, art, commerce, or politics. Most of us, though, the prudent and hard-working bearers of old-fashioned morality and family values, often feel we have just been chosen to suffer. This is our sacrifice. We offer our involuntary suffering at the closed minds and blind hands of the world's great and small tribes over the ages so they can develop more light—albeit very slowly and, for us, much too painfully. But everything under the sun unfolds in an endless chain. Its living rings are connected by the interdependent duality of cause and effect. There are no accidental events in that chain ...

"Therefore it is not accidental that it was, bodily, one of us, a hard-working visionary carpenter, who consciously sacrificed himself in a torturous death, so his sermon on love given on the Mount of Olives could be heard by the masses over centuries, and his powerfully forgiving silence on the cross remembered. He suggested through his sacrifice that learning to love others could indeed become an evolutionary possibility for *humankind in its entirety*.

"Alas, this superficial world tends to focus, too often with bitter envy, only on that spectacularly successful fraction of us. In such scrutiny, it would be better to see the weaknesses of ego and error that all human beings harbour. Sadly, too little recognition is given to the great contributions that select few have added to civilization's progress and accomplishments.

"We, the plain builders of this unprecedented invisible monument belong, with notable exceptions, to that unsung majority of our old and homeless tribe. We once lived as ordinary people: bakers, teachers, tailors, carpenters, clerks, labourers, musicians, retailers, doctors, craftsmen, farmers, and many others. We were just normal, sentient beings like everyone else. Naturally, amongst all people inhabiting Earth, the accomplished sainthood is rare. We represented every imaginable trade and always worked very hard, never being better off than those we lived amongst. Yet, after following us so faithfully for so long, the lightning of suffering did strike. Not once, not twice, but many times. Our vibrant, loving families were brutally uprooted. Then we were transported without food or water to unknown destinations in worse conditions than cattle heading to the slaughterhouse. Finally, we were passed through torture chambers, on our way to anonymous deaths, from which we have given ourselves to the mysterious body of the universe.

"Passing through those poisonous gas chambers of impenetrable, suffocating hatred, we offered our blood and sweat to the similarly wandering element of water, our tormented bodies to the likewise fierce element of fire, our thick, black smoke to the equivalently landless and invisible element of air, and our fine white ash to the also terrified soil. Our amassed suffering grew beyond description and qualification, beyond word and thought. It could only be vicariously—and barely—touched by the instrument of human love in this monumental silence, in the sound bytes of suffering that we have left behind.

"Rare indeed is such warm feeling towards us who perished on the enormous sacrificial altar to humanity's spiritual growth. Too many people, including some religious leaders, have sadly forgotten about the millions of us. Shall we once meet a special pope in the purest of white, who after vacating the Vatican's most famous of windows in Rome, would greet us here, with his unforgettably stretched arms, and smiling, offer a loving shalom? Then say – 'how could I not visit our older brothers?'"

"While suffering, we did not know as to why, shocked to numbness by the utmost injustice wielded by our oppressors' black hole of blind hate. The warriors among us took up arms and fought back. Then others, less oppressed than us, came and joined our fight shoulder to shoulder. That, we will never forget. Many such souls came from the cloudy land where the monument to our suffering stands, one beyond the material world. The weakest souls betrayed us all, bowing to the lord of darkness and his blind, fear-ridden, hateful servants. We have forgiven what will nevertheless always be remembered.

"Some rabbis, suffering along with the rest, have suggested that our extermination must have had some definite meaning, even if beyond our understanding. Yet we did not know that the bricks of our martyrdom were erecting a moral and material monument to the genocide of the Holocaust, a silent dome with the mission of warning humanity. For *we* suffered from terrible fusion of modern technology with obsessively orderly organization that raised the fuel of sheer hate to a new level of legally sanctioned sadism, something *sub-barbaric*.

"We also did not fathom that out of our excruciating pain we would build the future home for our ancient and decimated tribe. This new nation on the old swath of land, Israel, recognized now like any other country, immense in spirit, if tiny in mass. Its flag's colours, whether the blue and white stripes of our death-row clothing, or the blue of the Mediterranean skies and the white of Jerusalem's Wall of Tears, defines all that we are. Our tribe has returned after centuries of painful wandering, to live in peace. We will our hopes and wishes to make it so. But we have always been … the chosen ones.

"We have suffered under enslavement by Egyptian pharaohs, occupation by the Roman Empire, segregation in medieval ghettos, and more. Most diabolical of all, we have recently suffered massive genocide in the concentration camps of modern Europe. Surrounding our tribe through history like a pack of grim wolves around a flock of sheep have been targeting us ignorance, with its anti-Semitic knife of hate.

"Now, our legacy stands alone, potentially facing eye to eye an innumerable adversary. Some in the world still call for total annihilation of this small tribe, at times calling them to fight again for their right to exist. Understandably, they are most sensitive to brewing dangers and highly motivated to address them early, refusing ever again to resemble the defenceless sheep. To be sure, no mortal fight—ugly by definition—ever appears indispensable or emotionally bearable to an unaffected observer living in relative safety. However, when the danger is knocking on one's *own door*, taking up arms instantly gains an enticing righteousness.

"Ultimately, the Jewish people know they have to count on themselves. Their friends could weaken any time, their moral or material strength suddenly dwindling under pressure. Alas, very few came to the rescue when *we*, their ancestors were robotically exterminated by the Nazi state-terrorists, who managed to hypnotize and terrorize the fear-frozen masses in Europe.

"Who would there be to come to the rescue, if and when future waves of hypnotized or terrorized people attempted to push our living brothers and sisters into the sea? They live daily mindful of that possibility, hoping never to be forced to exert the full power of their desperation, turning it to steel. Steel hardened in the fire of Nazi ovens and cooled in the ominous smoke they will *never ever forget* …

"Now we, the ghostly reflection of that tiny nation in the calm elsewhere, pray for a miracle, since we know that they do happen: *Adonai, please bestow upon them a miracle of civility, understanding, and the warmth of friendship from other nations. Let there be lasting peace. For only such a miracle would prevent the world from an apocalyptic lightning. But if the lightning must come, we pray that whatever mysterious force that long ago* chose *this old tribe would arrive on time and shorten the trying period, as was once promised in writing.*

"*We humbly pray that the world comes to understand what unbearably hard decisions, made under the most extreme conditions, are faced by the establishment there. And that its human mistakes are scrutinized with sober compassion. We pray also that all the world be granted the wisdom to perceive at last the human right to self-government by all common Israelis, and not merely see a political system to oppose or support, as politics come and go, whereas a nation of people remains—unless annihilated. We pray that the other nations of the world opt to support and protect all persons of Jewish descent dispersed amongst every country of this blue planet, against the menace of anti-Semitism. And that it chooses to remember us with sympathy, we who keep reaching out towards this world from another realm.*

"We are your late brothers and sisters, ordinary people just like you, many of us little boys and girls, inexplicably chosen to suffer, the mirror reflection of our earthly twins living now on a narrow strip of arid land. Like once we were, they contemporarily are labourers, bakers, teachers, tailors, carpenters, engineers, retailers, clerks, doctors, janitors, artists, farmers, students, and many more. Together we build this monument to human martyrdom to protect the future. But we need help to do so.

"From this inherently impartial *elsewhere*, we have placed an invisible shield above their increasingly endangered heads. We construct it from our love, which is all we have. Yet we also need the love of other tribes to make the shield invincible, to complete it in time. We invite all *independent, brave souls* amongst you, whose thinking encompasses the full scope of the planet, to come and join us with your warm and open hearts and minds in mental and spiritual solidarity to complete this shield—before it's too late."

Victor sat upon the wooden bunk, blinking the sleep from his head. *Something has happened.* He watched the shy sunbeams begin their slow enlightenment of the eclipsing darkness, making the space around him seem that much more puzzling. It would take him years to understand what this night had brought him. What these indefinable sound bytes were saying, or what these feelings were that they produced in him with their painful melody played on instruments that did not exist in his world. All he knew was that something unusual—spectacular even—had happened here.

He resolved to study human life in all its intricacies, both positive and negative, and spend his lifetime on this self-commissioned task. Victor would experience the hard life first and examine it in his own way. He embarked for some years on that gruelling, but interesting educational quest. The gothic corridors of the city's venerable university with such former students as Copernicus and teachers as John Paul II would have to wait for Victor, ever struggling with his various limitations. Working as a plain labourer and immersing in varied social classes, he was ensuring that he would never be one to study the mystery in human life from behind a pundit's desk.

One sunny afternoon, before graduating from high school, he was walking to a less-than-savoury bar to meet three of his new friends from the cement factory that will eventually employ him. They wanted him, a sturdy youngster, on their paid-on-commission team. Victor had been studying recently the words of some ancient Chinese philosophers. One of them wrote, "Every third person you meet in life is your teacher." The philosopher explained that the positive teachers show one whom to become, the negative ones whom *not* to. Entering that crowded bar, Victor looked at the seemingly uncomplicated faces of his three older friends, and a thought crossed his mind, *Who of them will become my teacher?* He recalled that previous mental alert that had sent him to his night in the seemingly lightless and allegedly empty barracks at Birkenau. The stark, forgotten structure, quietly hosting its own agonizing musical-like passage, once composed into the powerful, forever cryptic symphony of silence.

What was in store on this occasion? Victor thought. He decided to wait and see before he joined their team. Independent intellectually, as well as emotionally self-sufficient for a youngster, he liked to do what he wanted with these days of his youth. He had always been this way. Presumably, he would be able to do what he pleased with his entire, slowly unveiling life. After all, he was not afforded the luxury of having supervision ... or so he thought.

A Syndrome of Otherness

—In memory of Emil Rosenzweig, MD, Holocaust survivor

After those man and woman in love
Have emerged from that bland legion of all others
To become my own father and mother,
I've started developing
The long-term, full-blown illusion
That they had never belonged to the "just-others"
From whom they have clearly come

My future wife had also belonged
To the vast camp of those others,
The same from which I came, surprisingly to her,
So we could get married too happily
Until—she passed away
Hence the camp of others offered me a new wife

It looks like I've been suffering from a Syndrome
Of Otherness for my entire life
How far does it go? Were my bloodline ancestors
Beyond the great-great grandparents
Whose names I know only—others or non-others
Back, to the ice age caves?

The matter is even more complex since some others
Proved their ability to shape-shift readily
Becoming then the non-others,
Like old Doctor Emil who one day saved my life
A gravely ill child,
Or that time-buried wise author
Who showed me the exit in the maze of youth

What about that master baker whose artisan bread
I've often enjoyed much?
The firefighters who won the battle with flames
Too close to my house,
Or soldiers who may in the future put themselves
As the very first
Between me and the danger,
Do they belong to that blended group of "others,"
Or should they be seen as the distinct "non-others"?

It increasingly appears that the others may not exist
But even if they somehow do,
They are not really foreign to me and distant others ...

Let's rush to love others as they are, forgiving that no better, no prettier they seem to us, as we seem to them ...

—Jan Twardowski, priest-poet

Our True Colours

Embracing the other ones is not a "rose garden"
As we subconsciously tend to find in them
Precisely, what we most dislike in ourselves,
With them reliably never much postponing
To reciprocate in kind, and too aptly as well,
Making us feel hurt, so in a reflex we hurt back

Yet, *we could see them* as most impermanent
Sent by fate seafaring mates, poor sailors like us,
With whom we share the deck pre-assigned once
In the blue spacecraft that we soon leave behind

It's after we gave the souls of a journey's mates
To the sea's magnetic waves fast burying them,
That we are haunted by thin blades of regrets
Seeing modest belongings they used—now left
As something cries in us, finding it's too late
To show our *true colours, while sailing with them* ...

The Two Last Regrets

Irrespective of culture, religion, and race,
Those who have returned to us
From being guided in grey tunnel of clinical death,
All have insisted
In their diversified languages
That when the chilly insight of "not coming back"
In-silence dawned on them,
The beyond description regret
Felt twofold

They were in pain discovering
That it now will be forever impossible for them
To become gentle to others
Left behind on Mother Earth,
And felt profoundly sorry that never
Would they be able access all the knowledge
They could have acquired,
Had they on time applied themselves
While on Earth

Adjusting for the diehard sceptics,
At least what the global comparative field-studies
Have confirmed and re-confirmed
Beyond even a slight doubt ...

The Wall of Tears

Self-forming in agony, this garden in blue and white,
Had cried for time immemorial
Spilling out the soft streams of its ruby-hot magma

When the time of sorrows had wisely reduced itself
To echo, in the psalms of King David,
The Earth has, in relief, left her graven tears behind

Her soft tears have turned to stones in various colours,
Got spilled all over young continents,
But the Earth did offer her mourning shade of white
Only to the noble Wall of Tears …

The Wall of Tears, built of the whitest tears on Earth,
Now calls silently the chosen ones
Still wearing the complementary black, round hats,
While murmuring prayers in front of it

It appears to be one, of their compounded reasons why
They gently rock slender bodies sunk in auras
Eclipsed by the bluest sunshine,
In-trance bowing towards the in-white, crying reverie.

On the Crossroads

This is a unique spot
In which an old Soviet accordion could play
The zesty "Hava Nagila"
In a kolkhoz-nostalgic way,
Or a young, vibrant voice could sing it
Sephardic-like, joyfully

In this place like no other
The taste of East-European cabbage rolls
Blends with hot spices
From the east and south,
But the black and white
Remains solemn
In a smiling rainbow of the younger colours

This is the holy land
Where all directions come to a crossroad,
As once upon a time they did
For the three kings,
Who saw high above the nest of Bethlehem
A stripe of sky with a yellow star

The Golden Dome

Golden dome—
Are you an ancient spell—engraved into stony walls,
Built to support your shine,
Or a scroll destined to open the walls of human minds
One written in pure gold,
Sagely put in a clay jar of the holy city of Jerusalem?

Golden dome—
Are you the most sacred vortex, for planetary transit,
To first come your way,
When the stars from discord towards harmony realign,
Or the bright symbol, worrisome
Of the mindsets facing a climax in their unfolding strife?

Golden dome—
Are you the most enduring from myths-in-the-making
For the future of humankind,
Or a lightning rod
For the burst of light by the Mediterranean gold-spear sun
Readying to pierce,
This transient shield of now,
To cut the path for the insatiably hard glory yet to come?

Our Temples

The true function of each, on Earth, erected temple,
Likely built of more than Earth's matter
Is to serve as a miniature bridgehead for the Ideal—
In an overwhelmingly material world

All temples, through varied architectural designs,
Point towards the clouds above,
Approximating the abstract concept of the beyond
That stays neither vertical nor horizontal

Their strikingly diversified contours
Reflect the soul of epochs' religions and cultures
The affluence of potent founders,
And the craftsmen's finest visions borne to art

Many prefer to regularly attend them
To confirm their faiths' affiliations, thus feeling safer;
Some visit them at such times
When the silent voice compellingly calls

The awe-invoking spell of shrines built by mankind
Blends with the splendour around them,
Implying that the material world
May be seen as sheer temple, for all sparks of divine ...

Compassing that path, circuitous we journeyed ... till at the point, whence the steps led below.

—Dante Alighieri

Three Questions from Silence

Has been this no-exit journey in the maze of "material,"
(Embarked on by all, who haven't found, yet,
The awaiting in life tranquility Grail),
Possibly, been your long-echoing cry for help?

Do you love to watch calm waters, inviting sunsets
To gaze at the leisurely burning
Sparkling wood, in tamed flames,
Look at the gently waving wheat fields,
Follow the barely passing soft shapes of still clouds?

Has the search for serenity been infused in your blood
From genes, or has it forever slumbered
Within this in circles travelling, yet still homeless soul?

Part II

Garden of Light

Virtue, like a strong and durable plant, may take root and thrive in any place where it can lay hold of an ingenious nature.

—Plutarch

Forgiveness

Forgiveness is a fragrant herb
With miraculous powers,
Brought to this cold world
Through the fine-tuning ability
Of each born-again planter,
That with the enlightened distance looks
At the so-very-own
And all too often excruciating past ...

The easier part of this hard process
Is to truly reconcile,
At least in one's memory,
With all those conspicuous others
Who through their blind actions
Left one deeply wounded,
Marked with never-to-vanish hidden scars,
And receive the grace
Of peace in the closure of forgiving

The next more difficult stage
Involves the wise courage of reopening
One's own skeleton's closet
With the "forgotten" past personal mistakes
By which back then
Some others have become
So mindlessly and profoundly hurt,
And from the depth of remorse
Receiving the grace
Of also forgiving oneself

Only after forgiving those blind others
And forgiving even oneself,
The miraculous powers of this sacred herb
Are born to the world to change it ...

The passers-by, who looked at this old man walking down the very crowded
street in India, thought that he must have been a professional soldier in the

past, perhaps for a long time. His posture was ramrod-straight, and he walked in that fast, even, self-assured way. The man was lean, with broad shoulders and strong arms. Even his distant but focused eyes could have been described as a sharpshooter's. Even much younger men would likely not want to mess with him. He wore a grey beard and a turban that towered above the heads of the street's crowd. This tall old man must be a Sikh.

First impressions can be right. Yoginder was indeed a retired, highly decorated, sergeant major of the Indian Armed Forces. Moreover, in his long-term military career, he served in several combat zones as a sniper. True to its owner's calling, Yoginder's Lee-Enfield repeating rifle did have an impressive line of small marks … But all that pertained to the past. Now, he remained idle, having closed a grocery shop, his second career after leaving the army. Yoginder had a lot of time on his hands now, and he was not quite sure how to spend it. He was a widower, with no children, and had good reasons not to be close to his brother and sister. Anyway, they did not live in Punjab, where he had a small, orderly, and clean apartment. It was comfortable for him, adorned by some of his war memorabilia, as well as a diploma with a picture signed by a long-dead white-clothed minister of defence.

In order to feel active, he tended to walk the streets of his once pleasantly sleepy town, rather than sit, like some of his peers, philosophically watching life from the battered benches. Although he was generally observant of his religion, frequently attending the local shrine, that did not necessarily work for him either. So, he patrolled his district almost daily, registering the changes in his neighbourhood. Most of them were not to his liking, bringing more noise and unnecessary traffic. He was brought up with strict morals, therefore Bollywood's colourful posters with the increasingly under-dressed actresses tended to cause him to frown. So did their spineless, clean shaven, effeminate screen-lovers. Would such a spoiled, soft-handed toy boy even be *able* to defend his country if he should be called in a time of need?

Yoginder had three close friends, but they were usually busy with their many grandchildren. It was all right. He was taking his relative solitude in a non-sentimental, quite factual way. After his long but brisk walk today, he returned to find an unexpected letter in the mailbox. It came from Rajastan where his brother lived on a family farm. As far as his older brother was concerned, Yoginder considered him to be a lowly thief. He had not talked to Mahesh for decades.

During his first combat deployment, before Kashmir, Yoginder fought the Chinese army high up in the Himalayas in 1962, defending the area of Arunachala-Pradesh. Although his army was taken by surprise and took a beating there, he did not. He decided to stay behind his retreating platoon to slow the Commies down. He returned very lightly wounded with three new marks on his rifle. It was during that bitter campaign that his brother, Mahesh, persuaded their aged parents to sign some papers. Not understanding, they changed their will, disowning Yoginder and his younger sister. The large farm went to the older brother when they passed.

At first, Yoginder wanted to throw the letter in the garbage. Perhaps due to some curiosity, or simply not having much to do, he opened it, angrily. His brother was asking his forgiveness for being greedy and stealing from Yoginder his inheritance. Mahesh was critically ill and begged him to come before he departed the world. He had something very important to tell his younger brother. Yoginder always harboured a sense of duty and that sense urged him to respond. By afternoon, with mixed feelings, he was sitting on a train heading towards Rajastan and thinking, *What would it be like to see his brother after such a long time? What would they even say to each other?*

These questions proved to be unnecessary. Before he made it to the village, his older brother, Mahesh, passed away. Their sister did not come from the more distant Karanataka. Yoginder took part in the very modest, sombre funeral arrangements, cooperating with his sister-in-law and her family as best he could. Everyone tried to be nice, but he noticed them avoiding his eyes. It felt like they would be happier seeing him return to Punjab sooner rather than later. Before leaving, he asked the widow, "What was it that my brother wanted to tell me?" She said she did not know. No one saw him off to the bus.

Riding on the train again, he watched white flocks of birds taking off from the fields. His parents—and now his brother—had taken off like them. Mahesh had taken with him all he wanted to tell his younger brother … *What was it?* Anyway, he must have cared about Yoginder before he left, otherwise he would not have written, and would not have insisted on conveying something to him later, in person. Perhaps for the first time in his adult life, Yoginder felt that something in his internal being had loosened. It used to be resilient as a bunker. He knew enough about how hard it was to break bunkers, having busted a couple with clusters of hand grenades in combat. His own internal bunker seemed to be opening by itself. But to what he did not know. Without much intellectual elaboration, he knew there was no grudge in him against Mahesh anymore.

Rather, as his brother had asked for forgiveness in the letter, it would be appropriate to give it to him. He said quietly, so the other passengers would not hear, "Mahesh, I forgive you for what you did in a moment of weakness. In fact, I do not even remember what you have done now. You've been a good brother to me, rest in peace." He felt lighter, and unexpectedly, younger. This was a new experience indeed.

After returning home, he kept thinking about his younger sister, Maya.

Until now, he had felt that she and her husband had impudently crossed him. He held a deep grudge against her too-brainy hubby, with whom he had not been on speaking terms since before the war. Yoginder was to be deployed to Kashmir, and travelled to Bangalore to say goodbye to his sister. He never liked her husband, Prem. He was a nerd, with thick glasses, a high-pitched voice, and a fancy education. Of course, Prem did not plan to defend his country.

The goodbye evening morphed into a political discussion. Yoginder felt that his brother-in-law offended the army with his smart-alec pacifist remarks. As for himself, he was a part of that army because of his own genuine choice, and he felt deeply hurt by the insulting words of a man whom he'd disliked from the beginning. Yoginder was about to go to war, putting his life at risk, but the man sloughed him off, dismissing his potential sacrifice. Enraged, Yoginder swung and gave what he thought was a light slap to Prem's face. But the weakling fell on the floor, unconscious! Horrified, Maya cried out and never spoke to him again. Someone called the police and Prem was rushed to the nearest hospital. Where he enjoyed a brief stay—*a holiday*, thought Yoginder.

Yoginder had never analysed that quarrel more deeply. But his memory was good, and now he reconstituted their conversation. The only thing he could recall Prem saying, while raising his voice in some agitation, was "I wish that all the armies would not be necessary once!" Sure, it was insensitively idealistic to say that to someone who, driven by a patriotic duty, was about to go to the frontline. Nevertheless, it was certainly not enough to put a man in the hospital for a couple of days. Moreover, he was his brother-in-law, after all. Clearly, Prem was not only physically hurt, but worse, badly humiliated in front of his younger wife. Suddenly, Yoginder did not feel good about that past event at all. He wrote Prem a short letter with just three laconic sentences. "Prem, I confess with regret that I did not like you in the past, but I know that you have been a good husband to my sister for all these years. Forgive me please for hitting you. I do feel sorry that I put you in the hospital back then."

The answer came with no delay. "Dear Yoginder, We are happy that you wrote, and forgave you a long time ago. What I said at that emotional time, I should have kept to myself. I felt horrible about you being soon in combat, and dreaded that you may lose your life. Now we are retired too, but we have a large house in a nice, mature garden. Please spend as much time with us as you can. We would be delighted to have you here."

Yoginder did not write back for the time being, but he felt better about everything, with his own stern life in particular. He made a list of people he felt he could apologize to for some past wrongs. And he wrote them, making his amends. Most of them did not respond, but one letter he received was of great value to him. He once put to court-martial a soldier under his command for his cowardice in combat. That young man was to be executed by firing squad. On the last day of his life, the court-martial commuted his sentence when medical evidence surfaced about the illness that was altering his sight. The soldier wasn't a coward, he was half-blind.

Yoginder's letter had asked for forgiveness from his family, as the ex-soldier was no longer alive. His son answered, "My father was a brave man and wanted to fight for his country, but the worsening problems with his vision precluded him from shooting. Eventually he became fully blind. He always respected you, saying that you were the only sergeant in the entire battalion who consistently led by example. My father knew that you just did not understand his deteriorating medical condition. He never held any real grudge against you."

This letter brought back many memories from their campaign in the exhilarating mountains and valleys of war-torn Kashmir. At that time, Yoginder was young, tough, and unforgiving to the enemy—promoted to master corporal right on the battlefield. Among many good and horrible memories, one related to a box where he kept a few souvenirs and trophies from that campaign. There was a black-and-white picture of a man and a woman, a small green book in Arabic, and a thin package with an unopened envelope, slightly browned by some very old traces of blood.

Yoginder put the packet on the table and looked at the old picture. At first, at the beautiful face of the unknown woman, and then at the manly but open face of the familiar young man wearing a black moustache. The entire scene came back to him as though it was yesterday. His troops needed to rest and re-supply after a counteroffensive. The Pakistani troops withdrew towards the further mountain range, but no one knew how far. Yoginder volunteered to scout, so the superiors would know what to expect before possible further pursuit or required defence. He was an experienced sniper and did not mind hunting down the enemies of his country, even if it meant he would be sometimes fighting alone.

He checked on his modified Lee-Enfield, took some additional supplies, and left during the night. Walking cautiously, he soon spotted some destroyed armour that had been left behind and several bodies of enemy soldiers. That did not bother him. He was glad that they would not walk the Kashmiri soil anymore. After some time he took a rest, made notes on his map, and began climbing uphill. Suddenly his well-honed combat instinct alerted him to proceed extremely carefully. Scanning the rugged terrain in the dim light of dawn, Yoginder slowly ascended towards the hilltop, a good observation point.

Not unexpectedly, he heard a gunshot, and a bullet chipped a piece of a rock right above his head. He saw an enemy soldier aiming at him at very close range. But that soldier was no match for a professional marksman. Even the Pakistani's fierce war cry "Allahu Akhbar!" could not help him. More experienced and always composed, Yoginder pulled the trigger first, and the enemy fell. Just in case other troops were around, he waited for gunfire, but nothing happened for a good while.

Yoginder carefully approached the fallen soldier. He was a man of roughly his age. Even though an enemy, he wore an identical British-designed helmet to Yoginder's, and also was armed with the same infantry rifle, but without the telescope.

No doubt mortally wounded, the young combatant was yet still alive. Yoginder took his rifle and checked for other weapons. The enemy soldier was now unarmed and at his mercy. After looking around, the victor saw a narrow, dark cave. Inside it, another Pakistani soldier lay on a blood-soaked blanket, unconscious and likely dying from an older, serious wound. He had a fresh bandage on his belly. There was also a metal cup by his head with a little bit of water.

With growing disbelief, Yoginder started piecing this miniature military puzzle together. It looked like the soldier he had just shot had not retreated with his comrades. He must have decided to stay and attend to his friend. Did he want to protect him, or knowing that the wounded man would die, just planned to bury him properly in due time, and then try to join his platoon? Maybe his only motivation was that he simply did not want him to suffer completely abandoned by everybody. Yoginder returned to the protector. He carefully placed him in the cave beside his friend, knowing the next visitor to this remote cave would be lone Death.

He left the tragic scene puzzled. Would he attend to his own friend in a similar way? Would he shoot him, even most reluctantly, if such a hopelessly wounded friend asked for the mercy-kill, and then leave with his own troops? That could be the likely scenario. What made this Pakistani soldier defy any basic military logic? Regardless, he must have been a brave and loyal man. Yoginder was a true soldier by nature, and probably that was what directed him back to the cave. He poured his own water into an old, scratched metal cup, placed it between the two dying men, and put a basic bandage on his enemy's wound. Yoginder knew well that such crude medical aid was merely a right gesture on his part. Before leaving for good, he snapped to attention and saluted the bravery and loyalty of the man he killed.

The enemy soldier opened his eyes. He moved his hand to the pocket in his bloodied uniform. Then, he pointed at his enemy. Master-corporal Yoginder understood. He removed from the pocket an addressed envelope, a picture, and a small green book in Arabic. He knew the soldier was counting on him to send this envelope, probably to the female in the picture. But the war, then other wars, continued. Yoginder never fulfilled the wish of the dying man left to perish in the mountains together with his too-loyally-protected friend … Instead, he nicked the next mark on his sniper's rifle and forgot about the entire event.

Now here he was looking at the old picture again. It may have been a wedding picture—he sensed happiness in their eyes. There was that trust and joy in her face drawing his attention. Her face seemed to say, "If you ever get to know me, you will see how good a person I am." Yoginder thought that the man he killed could have been a very lucky one, if too briefly. A strange, though vague, feeling of guilt began to emerge. *Nonsense*, he said to himself. This man was just one among many enemies that you honourably killed for your country, in action. That's all there is to it. Yet, his new feelings could not be simply reigned in. Feelings just *are* … He started to think that at least he should try to fulfill the fallen soldier's last wish.

What a hopeless venture; so much time has elapsed. Yoginder contacted an acquaintance in Islamabad who confirmed that the address on the envelope—some small town close to Quetta in northern Pakistan—indeed still existed. *Could the addressee still be alive?* He sent a short letter, in English, to the same name and address, informing her that he had some memorabilia from a soldier fallen in the Kashmiri conflict of 1965. Improbably, an answer came. The widow wanted him to send them to her.

Not understanding why, Yoginder increasingly felt that he should ask that widow for forgiveness—in person—and deliver the memorabilia himself. His extraordinary emotional need defied all logic. Perhaps in a similar way as that soldier's need to remain with his dying friend had defied any logic … Yoginder struggled deep within himself to resist his impulse. It was a long gone war. And Yoginder felt that he had done his duty honourably. But it did not even matter that the other soldier had shot first. His new feelings were gradually overpowering his unimpeachable logic. He did not know what to do.

Under the circumstances, hesitant Yoginder asked his three best friends for advice. Two of them urged him not to embark on the faraway and likely dangerous journey to the northern region of Pakistan. They simply could not understand what had happened to the always predictably self-disciplined ex-sergeant. The third friend wanted to see the picture first. He looked at it in silence and then said, "I do not know what you should do. Just take some time and gently listen to your heart. If it tells you to go, do not listen to anyone, even me. Just go." He was the friend Yoginder always respected the most, and this answer explained why. He took his advice, pondering long and hard, and finally decided to follow his compulsion to travel to Quetta, deliver the package, and ask the unknown woman for forgiveness.

There he was again on a train, and then on a bus, and finally on a colourful and dangerously overcrowded truck, heading along the precarious road out of Quetta to a small mountain town. Everybody he met on this journey recognized him as a Sikh who apparently came from India. Some showed him a degree of hostility, both verbal and non-verbal, but most just watched him carefully. Strangely, he felt that some people even liked him; certainly they respected him for wearing his proscribed red turban in their area, thus being true to himself and his religion. These individuals offered him friendly smiles, as well as useful information. A few hospitably shared their modest food. Overall, he did not feel like he was entering enemy land. All these common people were just like those in his native country, which he once served with his blood.

In the small dusty town, someone directed him to a house on its outskirts. He knocked on the large, wooden door of a small compound built of baked mud bricks. He had that long-absent but well-remembered adrenaline-rush feeling he'd experienced before each battle. Yoginder had always been able to put such a feeling under control. A young man opened the door. He had a brand-new assault rifle in his hand. Pointing it at Yoginder, he shouted something in anger. Then a middle-aged man appeared and quietly said a few words to the young one, probably his son. He seemed to remind him that Yoginder was a guest. As such, he was under the protection of not only the hosts, but also of Allah. The young man grudgingly mumbled some pseudo-apology, gave the guest a dirty look, and disappeared. The elder host invited Yoginder in and offered him a cup of sweet green tea, a pastry, and nuts. He knew why Yoginder had come, but could not hide his surprise seeing him in their remote house, so far from Punjab. Yoginder admitted he felt the same. They both could reasonably communicate in English. It turned out that his host had once been in the Pakistani Army and had also experienced some combat.

After the politely shared refreshments, Yoginder could not find the courage to ask to speak to the soldier's widow, although he very much wanted to. Instead, he removed the thin parcel from his weathered military backpack and was about to pass it to his host, but, as if reading his mind, the man refused to take it. He led the old Sikh soldier further into the compound where the widow was sitting in an austere room on a colourful, hand-woven carpet, mending clothing. She was stunningly beautiful. Obviously old, she nonetheless retained her glamour. Overcome with shyness, her guest gave her the envelope, the picture, and the small religious book. She saw the bloodstain on the envelope and started crying.

Yoginder wanted to crawl under a stone. He looked at her thoughtful face and regretted that he had killed her husband. The woman opened the envelope and began reading the letter, but she could not finish. She put the envelope aside and closed her eyes, sobbing. Yoginder knelt in front of her and, with some emotional pauses, uttered in English, "It was me who shot your husband in battle. He was bravely protecting his wounded friend until the very end. I am profoundly sorry for what I've done. It was the sudden, dire situation of either him or me. That was our fate, the fate of soldiers … I am old now and do not have a lot of time left. Please forgive me … if you can."

She understood, but said nothing. Yoginder remained on his knees for a little while, praying, with his eyes closed, for the soul of her late husband. Apparently she did not wish to forgive him. He had his pride too. Yoginder was about to open his eyes, stand up, and leave the room when he felt her hand delicately touch his face. She was consoling him, silently caressing his grey-bearded face like a mother caressing the face of a child. Yoginder, unable to believe what was happening to him, began to cry also, ever so slightly—in his core, still a military man—but probably for the first time since he was a child. Tears slowly flowed down his expressionless face and grey beard; that bunker within him miraculously evaporated. There was nothing hard or heavy left of that tough bunker anymore, just lightness, infused with an emerging love towards life …

He collected himself and briefly stood at attention, saluting the widow of that fallen soldier just as he had saluted her young husband so many years ago in that rocky tomb. Afterwards, he respectfully bowed and then left, without a word. The middle-aged man saw him off, but before they parted, said with sad warmth, "Thank you for taking the time to make this long, hard journey to our home, and bringing back my father's letter. Go in peace."

Upon returning to his increasingly noisy town, Yoginder knew what to do with the remaining time in his life. To the genuine surprise of the people who thought that they knew him well, he began volunteering in the local prison. Asked why, he explained that previously he had despised the offenders for breaking the law. However, after his very special travel to a certain remote house in the far-off mountains, he had learned the virtue of forgiveness must come to every human being, in due time, at some particular point in the chain of their lifetimes. "No human being is perfect," he said, "but there is a perfectly designed road … towards perfection."

Before his self-disciplined passage in the rudimentary local hospital, Yoginder served for years as a respected volunteer. He became known in the Punjabi corrections facility to be "firm but fair" with those who broke the law. He taught them by example, never being taken for granted by any of them. Despite his stern appearance and his characteristic no-nonsense, sometimes abrasively frank approach, the criminals liked him. Without knowing it, they felt attracted by the invisible, warm inner light that gradually expanded in him and around him.

Gratitude

Gratitude, the finest of internal arts,
Resembles composing, then practicing
One's own soundless music,
That calls to be consistently rehearsed
For the benefit of others,
And one's depth-tuning harmony

Gratitude creates its healing melody
For humans' ailing lives,
Offering them the miracle-treatment
That, if daily followed,
Before long gently dissolves
Emotional blood clots of unfounded fear ...

Plausibly, as long as one
Vests a calm mind into a clear heart,
Keeps awaking the power of gratitude
That slumbers in every soul,
There never a gate opens
For the darkly-bleak outer dissonances

Such devoted daily practicing
Can give birth to an unknown virtuoso,
Who from dawn to dusk
Replays that music to silence offered,
Grateful to the source
Of the unseen stream which offers life

What came first, the egg or the hen? In the same vein, has life been unfair to
Felipe or has he been unfair to it? What really mattered was that he did not feel
good about himself—or his sour life. Recently, Felipe's self-oriented thoughts
were growing progressively pessimistic. At times, he nearly sensed them as
either grey or black in colour. In a parallel way, his feelings either appeared to
be coldly numb or would, all of a sudden, become uncontrollably unfrozen.
If that happened, they would almost invariably dwell on the negative side of
the emotional spectrum.

    As his words and behaviours naturally followed those gloomy thoughts and feelings, eventually his family and friends stopped bothering to even try to reach out to him. Instead, they increasingly felt like sharing their little sorrows and joys with someone more rewarding. Felipe responded by withdrawing even more. No wonder he has felt pervasively unhappy for such a long time now. He's grown helplessly hopeless, as if separating from others by a slowly but surely thickening wall.

After a particularly punishing, ugly day, he had a puzzling dream. Someone came to him and briefly said something of utmost importance. This alerting feeling of importance and urgency suddenly woke him up. It was still dark outside. Only the very first pink-red lining enhanced the silvery horizon. He looked towards that gradually expanding harbinger of the day to come, attempting to recall who had come to him, and what they'd said.

His strained mind was on the verge of discovering it, but somehow could not cross certain subtle and elusive barriers. Perplexed, Felipe began realizing that, in a strange way, something had quietly changed. He was not able to pinpoint what this change was all about. Was it his surroundings that had become intangibly altered, or had it been an equally intangible difference occurring within himself?

He got up and, as he did every morning, he made a cup of coffee. A new thought crossed his mind—simply that its taste and fragrance were rich and pleasant. Curiously, Felipe also liked its warm, well-defined, dark colour. For some reason, he began thinking warmly about all the unknown people whose work had step by step brought this aromatic liquid to his comfy kitchen table for him to enjoy. What would he sip in the morning should that social chain leading to his small kitchen suddenly break? And what about his favourite, old coffee mug with the dreamy face of Marilyn Monroe on it? Clearly there were once some craftsmen, whose know-how enabled Felipe to cherish this beautiful mug, bought in the border town of Nogales, for years. Surely he could not make it himself.

And for that matter, how would he produce this worn out but still colourful plate he'd just put his warmed empanadas upon? They were made late last night by his wife, Rosa, whom he barely talked to anymore. Felipe had gotten used to thinking of her as a difficult and, quite frankly, unattractive woman. Until this particular morning, he had not thought much about Rosa's work, and even less so about her deep-fried empanadas. They were always there, taken for granted—like the air for his lungs—together with her tasty tortillas, burritos, chimichangas, enchiladas, all those hearty soups and succulent cakes of hers. So much to be amazed by!

His less-than-discretely aging wife was still sleeping soundly, after having cleaned the downtown offices until very late evening. For the first time since their once-promising youth, he gazed at her with his heart and eyes. Long-forgotten feelings he could barely define re-emerged and touched him. Felipe was readily discovering that he liked these new feelings slowly growing in him, empowering and soothing as they were.

Felipe had some time this morning before he had to take the crowded bus to the factory that had employed him for twenty years. He sat for a moment on the worn stoop of their modest house, nicely accented by lush oleander and bougainvillea bushes that a young and slim Rosa had planted years ago. A hummingbird sat nearby on the rusty wire of their old fence. Felipe looked at that common bird, really seeing it for the first time. He noticed the purple collar on its neck, harmonizing with the darker feathers of the wings. It occurred to him that this tiny and beautiful bird, though fragile and short-lived, was a brave creature in spite of everything.

Unhurriedly walking to the bus stop, Felipe suddenly experienced a mixture of lightness and optimistic curiosity, somewhere in the truest part of him; a feeling he had known very well once. Often he had felt this way as a boy, walking the same dusty street on his way to catch the slow, open bus that would take him to school. His father, respected by all the neighbours and greeted as Senior Antonio, would see little Felipe off. His mother had passed away, much too early, way too young, and Felipe only vaguely remembered her. After some years, his father, too, died—in an accident on the job. The same run-down, unsafe factory Felipe worked at now.

All of a sudden he pictured his late father's simple and sincere face, his black moustache that emulated Clark Gable's. Just like his own father's, who'd had a moustache like Errol Flynn's—or maybe Errol Flynn had one like his. Felipe stopped and looked at his hands, as if looking at his father's always busy and strong hands. He could feel that phantom hand again holding his own, still a boy's hand. Again he experienced that warm feeling centering in his heart, and something wet stopped short from coming to his eyes. After all, he was a hombre. Men have to pretend that never happens to them. He pulled himself together. A macho must be macho. Otherwise, who would remain a macho on this spiralling down, crazy planet? Not those fat mariachis in their enormous, bogus sombreros, for sure.

Surrounded by yawning, brusque colleagues, he was soon heaving bags of cement onto the non-stop conveyor belt, dirty with the smelly grey powder. He used to dislike most of his co-workers—particularly that moron, Ricardo, with his too-small body and too-big mouth. While looking at him today, behind his repulsive I-know-it-all facade, Felipe noticed another Ricardo. A pathetically lost, recent divorcee, who escaped from his insecurity and (perhaps well-deserved) loneliness in a bottle of fiery tequila. To his own surprise, Felipe thought, *Why can't we have some tequila in our little garden patio together? If not, this aggressive, bar-hopping Ricardo will likely end up in the squalid local jail. Perhaps I could share a few of Rosa's empanadas with this funny dude too?* He smiled at Ricardo who, not knowing what to make of it, chose to feel like he was being laughed at. He uttered some nasty counteroffensive remark. *Well,* thought Felipe, *this invite will need to wait a bit, but it will happen sometime, looks like. Who knows? We might even become friends.* They did not live too far from each other, after all.

Upon returning home, Felipe looked at his hardworking wife Rosa in the new way he'd rediscovered that morning, as if his eyes had lost the shells that had long covered them. True, she was not pretty—by now fairly overweight, with varicose veins on her massive legs. No surprise, she was wearing her usual cheesy dress, with the loud and tacky butterflies that she loved so much. But where were his eyes before? Why could he not see how much plain, human goodness and quiet dignity her dark, tired eyes contained? Why on earth had he thought of her as such a difficult woman? Although she clearly was not born to be a crowd-pleaser, never a chitchatting "social smoothie"; one could always depend on her and her delectable homemade tortillas. Exact replicas of those her mother had taught her to make back in her old, impoverished village. They were reliably waiting for him on the clean kitchen table every night, with refried beans and homemade hot salsa. A bougainvillea flower perched in a Coca-Cola bottle filled with water beside them tonight.

Instead of sitting down as usual to gobble his meal with nothing said, Felipe warmly hugged his wife, again attracted to her. Awkwardly, he explained to her that all these long years she has been loved, and her daily hard work much appreciated. Flabbergasted, she looked at him but, predictably, said nothing. Yet, Rosa started to suspect something good must have happened to her clumsy and almost always grumpy husband. He had been aging way too fast, and for years was pathetically infatuated with that ugly, cheap mug, showing—who knows why—that long-dead gringo woman's face. But what could she do? Rosa had only him—their grown children lived far away in that unbelievably rich foreign country—so they had no choice but to experience their problems alone.

But it seemed to her that a new and mysterious quality had come to their tiny house, a welcome change. A religious person, she attributed what she sensed as the rising light in Felipe to the Virgin Mary of Guadeloupe's miraculous (if long overdue) intervention. After all, it was her, faithfully-visited-by-flies, colourful but fading picture, the only wedding gift from Rosa's very poor parents, that she hung above the bed on that bright day of their marriage. Felipe, usually more sceptical, was not so sure. Not being much of a church-goer, he nevertheless consulted Padre Esteban. Unlike most other priests, the old priest devoted his entire life to the poorest and sickest orphaned children and abandoned old people. Therefore, he was most highly respected, if not outright venerated, in their shabby but vibrant neighbourhood.

After hearing about the short dream that had elicited something new and positive in Felipe, Padre Esteban explained to him, with a slight smile, that what had happened may have been the temporarily bestowed grace of gratitude. It was probably a once-in-a-lifetime chance that had been given him. The padre further warned that this highly beneficial grace would not remain unless Felipe invited and tended it with respect and consistency, like one tends a new vineyard. It would only be with daily invitations, respectful greetings, and loving nurturance of the grace of gratitude that he could possibly retain it. Maybe he should try extending it towards others ...

Felipe felt that this wise and humble, poorer than poor padre was right on the money. He decided to follow his advice as much as he could. Remembering well how awful he had felt before, and feeling so good at present, he began consistently tending to his imperceptible, inner vineyard.

Soon enough, he started finding that the sublime feeling of gratitude was a cure for about any ailment in the complex process called human life. As long as he genuinely felt grateful—whether in general or for something specific—no negative feelings were coming his way, whether from within or from the outside. Moreover, no pessimistic, idly, self-absorbed, or unkindly self-centered thoughts were there to hamper his increasingly clear perceptions. Most surprisingly of all, these perceptions were showing him a transitory, ever-evolving, and precious reality.

Felipe's growing virtue of gratitude was becoming a major part of his inner life, bringing him as close to happiness as any fallible human being could be brought. Now he felt grateful in the morning towards the spectacularly rising sun, and towards the discretely shining moon in the unfolding night. He was grateful that trees happened to be green, that white clouds leisurely passed over blue skies, that a stray dog seemed to smile at him, or that an unseen bird sang for him. Foremost in his gratitude, the facts that his wonderful wife, Rosa, was alive, and they were still together. That's when he slowly began developing his gratitude towards the inexplicable reason for it all ...

Of course, the birds were not, as yet, flying to their tiny garden to sit on his arms so they could bask in the radiant halo around his balding head. Despite that, envious Ricardo had started sarcastically referring to him as "San Felipe." They had begun ending their weeks of hard labour by regularly munching on, among other succulent things, crispy empanadas enhanced with hot jalapenos, not without a shot or two of tequila followed by lime with salt. Ricardo's usual sarcasm, and his trademark emotional volatility, did not bother Felipe anymore. He knew by now that Ricardo liked him, but expressed his feelings in the only way available to his busy lips. So Felipe even felt grateful for the presence of a good friend such as Ricardo, who was now just teasing him in his and Rosa's cheap plastic garden chairs that had not been white for many years. These were Felipe's blessings in his unchanged, yet absolutely renewed life.

Moderation

Not the worldly reaches make a man great—but how he shares them with others.
—Pope John Paul II

Lost in the race, we might miss out on our promised land
One which does not await somewhere, afar and away

That asylum for the inner peace of too embattled souls
Is seen on some ancient maps as the Realm of Moderation

In its fertile valleys surrounded by the extreme peaks
The rivers of prudence and safety feed Harmony Lake

Legend has it that those tranquil and life-healing waters
Stay invisibly connected to the calm Ocean of Utmost Joy

They say only frugal settlers in that emerald, garden valley
Have a fair chance of discovering the mysterious passage

Many others tried to find it among the excessive summits,
But perished—left frozen in a variety of extreme postures

Adam met Eve not yet in paradise, but on the way to it. To say that they
fell in love at first sight would be an understatement. Their souls, expressing
themselves via Adam's dark and Eve's blue eyes, recognized in seconds the
multidimensional value they presented to each other. They instantly embraced
the rare gift that life or fate brings to some, usually in the most unexpected
moments.

Perfect strangers, they introduced themselves by saying "I am Adam" …
"I am Eve." Having exchanged such complementary names, they immediately
burst into laughter, showing an identical sense of humour. Their university
campus, studies, exams, and the unknown future temporarily dissolved in the
overwhelming joy of this crucial moment in their lives.

True, they were coming from entirely different social strata and
backgrounds, but it did not matter to them. Soon they both felt like sharing
their lives with each other, regardless of who said or did what. Predictably,
some strongly negative statements and even certain actions on the part of their
families followed, all intended to "open their eyes" before "making a huge

mistake." Yet, Adam and Eve had already made their choice. Fortunately for them, their characters shared a trait in common, beyond both being gentle. That charitably-disguised feature, their genuine firmness, was reminiscent of a coiled spring, made of the best steel. Given the depth of their connection, and that handy trait of character, no one had even a chance of separating them. They patiently weathered all the foreseen family storms, not without employing their good senses of humour, eventually graduated, and got married.

They subsequently entered the paradise that gladly awaited them. Not only did Adam and Eve happen to be born in a country accustomed to feeling rich, they also secured golden jobs, both being professional computer wizards. Not having too much debt after graduating, they could readily borrow the desired lifestyle. The relentlessly modeled patterns of such a lifestyle flowed towards them in an unending, colourful stream. It radiated from TV, movie screens, vibrant magazines, their ostentatiously successful bosses, co-workers, friends, and neighbours.

Several years after their twins, Rachel and Mary, were born, the family moved from their tiny bungalow to a prefab mansion. A team of angel-designers created for Adam and Eve a sprinkler-aided wonder garden. Another similar team blessed them with knowledge about what furniture must be put where, what pieces of art would work with this furniture, and what colours of paint, fixtures, and tiles would work with their furniture and art pieces. Topping it all with a swimming pool, games room, and a home-entertainment centre boasting a state-of-the-art home theatre, Adam and Eve finally completed their paradise ... except for the cars.

In their new neighbourhood, only certain makes and models of cars—the business card on wheels—seemed to work with the sprawling prefab mansions. Such vehicles had to be either expensive, imported sedans with some "sporty" attributions, or the chrome-friendly four-by-fours, elevated to look larger. The latter were, sort of, allowed to be domestic, but preferably not. Interestingly, in the nearby blue-collar neighbourhood, such social driving codes morphed towards huge, powerful domestic trucks. When one sat in these "monster cars," the seats were elevated even higher than in the shiny four-by-fours adorning the richer area. Adam went for a domestic SUV, with power everything. The more discerning Eve chose an imported convertible, one discretely creating the impression of a mature, somewhat artistic affluence. Making these proper choices, they confirmed their full-fledged membership in the gated paradise.

Over the next few years, after purchasing many other items, services, newer and newer gadgets, adequately referred to as "toys," they started to feel somehow anxious, perhaps becoming oversaturated in a difficult way to explain. There seemed to be no rationale for it. They were doing well in their jobs. Unlike most of their peers, they had managed to pay off a substantial part of their mortgage, recently increasing their payments, to the concealed frustration of their financial advisor. Their improved ties with their respective families were quite cozy by now. Adam and Eve were too young for a midlife crisis, and their bright, diligent daughters were about to enter a prestigious, private high school. Nevertheless, something undefined was starting to bother Adam and Eve more and more.

Both being intelligent and refined persons, they realized that perhaps the time had come to reinvent themselves. Eve knew what to do. Always interested in the arts, she quit her architect of computer systems job and opened a small art gallery. After some time, it became an enterprise with promise. Adam did not feel like quitting his job any time soon. He'd lately gotten promoted, now making even more money with his hefty, executive bonuses. He addressed his growing need for change by taking up tennis on top of the regular, obligatory golf-for-turf matches with his aging boys' club. Eve seemed to be growing happier than he. Sometimes he felt that she'd left him behind in a certain way. Nothing appeared to quell his elusive, internal restlessness, felt as quiet frustration, if not full-blown existential confusion.

Maybe as a result, Adam began enjoying his drinks a bit more than before. One uneventful evening, lost between the two distant ends of his enormous soft couch, sipping some scotch on the rocks, he turned on with a double clap of his hands the huge home theatre across the room. The delicate face of a small child appeared on the wall-sized screen. A certain charity was suggesting support for the education of orphaned children from third-world countries. He had seen the ads before, but although feeling vaguely sympathetic always, he'd never cared to write down a number. Now he took it down, not knowing what made this particular time different. Then he called it. Once he did that, Adam became a sponsor of one orphaned child, for the price of one dollar a day.

He soon received a picture of nine-year-old Ernesto from El Alto in Bolivia, along with some basic information about him. Ernesto's school progress reports came in the mail from time to time. Adam did not pay much attention to the facts of Ernesto's life, and did not feel motivated to read those reports, even though the charity translated them into English. He noticed, *en passant*, that Ernesto had taken a course in this language. However, the boy just seemed to exist as an abstraction. He was, after all, so far away.

Then one day, a letter came in which Ernesto, in broken English, wrote to thank Adam for his care. There was a new picture in the envelope. Thin, smiling Ernesto was standing, clearly very proud, in front of a small, one-story, pitifully squalid almost shack-like building. He wrote on the reverse:

"My school is big." It was at that moment when something changed for Adam. From a kind of pity for the boy and his pathetically dilapidated school, a feeling of human solidarity with him emerged and, with it, the motivation to protect him and that destitute school Ernesto was so proud of.

That unexpected letter caused Adam to begin developing some small degree of an emotional bond with Ernesto, a clearly intelligent boy from the indigenous Aymara tribe. Eventually, Adam started pondering whether or not to travel to El Alto and meet him. He felt that he *should* go there. Eve gladly supported the plan, surprised that Adam had taken an interest in someone else. Adam took a course in basic Spanish, allowing him to linguistically get by, and he read a little bit about Bolivia. A year later, he found himself on a LAN plane, flying towards the highest-elevated airport in the world, situated above the sprawling capital city of La Paz.

Adam was well travelled but so far had never seen a third-world country. He spent a few days in La Paz, a city that struck him as old-world nice, but visibly deprived. In the city's best hotel, everyone was genuinely polite, but it couldn't cover up the fact that one of elevators worked erratically. Walking in the evening, in spite of feeling safe himself, he noticed many people with small children sleeping in rows on the pavement. He gave five dollars to a Native South American woman with two little children. She looked at him in complete disbelief, as though he had just arrived from Mars. She was too shocked to even say thank you. After getting a feel for the capital, he took a battered taxi to nearby El Alto.

The town was restive, its chaotic roads often blocked by protesters, and it impressed him as a rough and poverty-stricken place. Still, he did not feel unsafe. It was just that the people kept looking at him with that expression of total disbelief. He was already learning to endure it. As he spoke some Spanish, and did not project an aura of superiority, it was not too difficult to find Ernesto's school. In person, it presented an even more miserable picture than in the photo. An astonished young teacher led Adam to a very small brick house with no running water. Ernesto lived there with a large, previously unknown family, paid by the charity to take care of the orphan.

Adam tried to talk to several adults, who all gave him that now familiar look. Someone went to call ten-year-old Ernesto home, as he was playing soccer—*fútbol*—with his friends. The family was destitute to the extreme, but nevertheless put a bowl of soup on the table for their guest. The other children stood around, gazing at him in the way that apparently came with the territory. He gave them a few candies, and that brought smiles to their faces. These smiles revealed incredibly white and very healthy teeth.

Then Ernesto opened the door, tired from playing soccer and running home as fast as he could. The boy approached Adam like he knew him, joyfully even. He was much more at ease than his slightly embarrassed benefactor. Adam did not really know how to greet him, so he simply put his hand on the boy's shoulder and commended him for good results in school.

Ernesto just smiled and answered in English, "I knew that you would be a very tall man. Do you play soccer?" With this question the boy bailed out the nervous Adam, who now had an opportunity to draw on a scrap of paper a tennis racquet and golf clubs. Then Ernesto happily—and proudly— showed him around. Afterwards, they talked quite a bit. Both trying to communicate in their respectively broken second languages, they more or less still understood each other. The boy said he dreamed of becoming a medical doctor in order to cure people. As his parents did not have a doctor or a cure, they had died, leaving him alone.

Soon Adam had to return to the taxi. He walked unhurriedly, accompanied by a sad Ernesto and feeling that his visit was not only surreal, but perhaps futile. Yet he also heard his inner voice suggesting that the visit would be futile only, if he let it be. Everything around was so unreal that he felt lost. Small Ernesto was almost more collected than he was. Adam knew that had the boy been born in his country, with the personality he had, he would excel and contribute his skill for the sake of others. But the boy was born in a drab village near El Alto, had no parents and extremely limited options. Adam gave him some farewell money and drove off in the taxi. The little orphan stood on the narrow, dusty street waving his hand for as long as he could see the motor car holding his extraterrestrial friend.

Upon his return to the suburban posh-paradise, nothing appeared quite the same. Adam began looking at his immediate surroundings from a different perspective. He noticed his SUV had unnecessarily large wheels, requiring huge, expensive tires. Sure, that arrangement gave him the pleasant sensation of sitting above the other drivers in a gridlock. Despite appearances though, the cabin was not really larger than a sedan's, except for the unnecessary abundant headroom. What about the array of expensive options with power everything that he rarely used? How about the largely dormant—thus frankly theoretical—power of two hundred sixty horses under the hood? Such horsepower, even if partially claimed, would surely secure a speeding ticket! Did he need to pay for all of that, plus the, on-average, double amount of gas required to run that engine, which relentlessly contributed to the smog above his fair city? Perhaps it had all been acquired just to feel good in comparison to other, less affluent drivers. As well as to fish for the acceptance of his socioeconomic peers, chasing the illusion of some alleged prestige. Now Adam thought about trading such costly, pollution producing prestige for the feel of driving a small, economical, and durable domestic vehicle that would get him from A to B.

What about the house? Before, he'd been proud of his huge staircase, the one advertised to be "continental-wide." Now, he felt as if he'd cheated himself. They'd paid so much for ... air. Each square foot of ... air ... cost the same as the actual living space, the split-level great room, the open-concept kitchen, and the five bedrooms and four bathrooms. At least there was a thin floor under a comparable ceiling. And the fragile gypsum drywall along with the studs of so-called two-by-fours were all pretty cheap. All snugly wrapped in an external corset of chipboard and vinyl siding against the increasingly unpredictable elements ... But here in front of him, was an enormous air pocket disguised as an open-concept, broken in the middle by this spectacularly expensive staircase, leading to the elongated side-balconies.

Ah, the bathrooms. They were using only two most of the time, but he'd paid for four, having been emphatically advised to upgrade by purchasing the highest-end imported fixtures for his low-end mansion's bathrooms. The vast kitchen would make quite an impressive boardroom, with minimal adjustments. After easily removing the taps, it would be enough to cover the long central island with a green cloth and add the respectable number of executive soft, leather armchairs. Why, just the entertainment centre downstairs was bigger than the entire house in El Alto. Wouldn't that house nearly fit into the magnificent "stroll-in" closet adjacent to the master bedroom?

Slowly but surely it had been dawning on Adam that he lived a self-absorbed, consumptive life in an artificial paradise, isolated from the majority of his brothers and sisters on a common blue planet with alarmingly dwindling resources. He tried to search into his mixed proud and uneasy feelings, but had difficulty pinpointing what bothered him most. Maybe it was guilt, but it was so vague ... it certainly was not only guilt. Perhaps a general feeling of disconnect ... yet not that exclusively either. Then there was this gradually emerging insight about the planetary context of his hitherto blissfully oblivious lifestyle ... Still, it did not strike a chord identifying it as the very kernel he searched for. Adam kept browsing his mind for that elusive factor that made him so emotionally uneasy.

Then, all of a sudden, his effort paid off. He was sitting in his handsomely stretched Jacuzzi, made of fake marble, holding a glass of champagne. Adam instantly laughed, comparing himself to Archimedes, who made his consequential discovery for physics also while taking a bath. Unlike Archimedes though, he discovered himself to be, in certain regards, a somewhat comical figure. For ambitious and highly intelligent Adam, a man gifted with innate integrity—that was it. A change had to come.

He recalled attending a bombastic social function, along with many other invited guests. His host, an actual stranger to him, sported gold-plated rails on his tycoon's top-of-the-line staircase. That palatial abode also boasted a wall-sized aquarium filled with a rainbow of tropical fish. Adam recalled whispering to Eve that the host might have been a bit pretentious, and perhaps … in a way … even an ethically challenged individual.

"You think?" she'd answered.

But how would someone poor, but intelligent and independently minded—say, from El Alto— perceive his own, smaller mansion? *Or him,* for that matter? Could what he had surrounded himself with—as well as his pride in doing so—make him a bit of a comical figure for an attentive observer on so diversified planet as this? Sure, less complicated individuals might envy him, but perhaps someone more schooled in the foibles of humankind, refined in perceptiveness, or cognitively independent might just laugh a little, seeing him lost in the soup of his faux-marble Jacuzzi with a glass of expensive champagne. Perhaps they could even grasp easily enough that he had borrowed the entire clichéd scene from a passé Hollywood movie—and laugh a bit more? Would they be curious enough to ask him how much he paid for his joyfully bubbling bath champagne?

Once Adam started analyzing his entire reality, social and ethical reality, he was seeing his role models and mentors through new lenses. He watched on TV an aged man, who wrapped himself in a hundred-twenty-foot luxury yacht. That elder was brazenly presenting every posh detail of his trophy to a smitten, young journalist. Adam kept laughing—was this mogul just a little bit comical, or comically tragic? But he also kept thinking about himself in this context. He increasingly yearned for an end to his role as a corporate executive, as a paradise-certified member of … of anything and anyone other than just true Adam again.

The time had come to talk to Eve about this still hazy, but emerging new vision for his … *their* future. For his decisions would affect hers and the kids' futures too. They talked for hours. He explained the affect Ernesto's picture had had on him initially. How his letter and photo had shaken him. And finally, how his visit to El Alto had changed him utterly. It surprised Adam to discover that Eve knew all this, even before he started explaining himself. She did not need to visit Bolivia to feel the same way; she had come to this on her own. As usual, they were on the same path as though synchronized by some gentle force.

Adam and Eve worked together to come up with a plan. Ever practical, Eve felt that they needed a transition period, during which they would iron out and correlate their evolving visions of a new life. The timing was right. Next year, their twins were to enter an Ivy League university far from home; the nest would become empty and feel even more spacious. Action-oriented Adam was listening to his inner voice. It suggested that he start donating 10 percent of his income to support the education of orphaned children around the world. Eventually, in addition to Ernesto, he would support Benjamin from Kenya, Sayed from Indonesia, Jaya from India, Bhopal from Sri Lanka, Leila from Egypt, Jose from Peru, Miriam from Rwanda, Robert from the Dominican Republic, and Chantal from Haiti. As these commitments did not exhaust his 10-percent tithe, he donated the rest to a clean water program in drought-beleaguered Sahel, Africa.

After their daughters left for university, Adam and Eve became ready to exit their paradise. They did not need any bank-angel to chase them out with the foreclosure's fiery sword. On the contrary, they pulled a bait-and-switch trick on that disappointed angel when the sale of their mansion brought them enough to buy a small property for cash. The modest leftovers assisted their studying girls, who also agreed to start working part-time in order to help themselves and learn about life in the process.

Adam chose to step off the executive platform of the success ladder. Now, much of his new staff-level job could be done from home via computer. His tithe would comprise more than 10 percent of his lower income, however, as he did not want to reduce the amount sent to "his children." Eve sold her gallery, which had become a profitable contributor to their joint income, and their luxury cars as well—with predictable losses. Bafflingly, leaving the gated paradise, they did not cry. Instead, they laughed.

Their next paradise was an orchard-embraced, compact, but quaint fixer-upper, with strong, pre-chipboard era walls. Tucked away on five rolling acres in the country, not too far from a small town, the house had three modest bedrooms and one bathroom. There was also some potentially cozy space for a studio in the attic. The kitchen was not spacious. However, it overlooked the apple trees—a far cry from their previous "boardroom-kitchen's" window that gazed upon the blind wall of the prefab mansion right next-door. They reduced their transportation options to a two-year-old Ford Focus with low mileage and a brand-new motor scooter. Adam planted a vegetable garden and tended their orchard in his new-found spare time. He gradually fixed up the house with his own hands, finding the activity both economical and pleasurable. Moreover, his few extra pounds disappeared with the country wind in no time.

Eve, who always liked herbs, started a herb garden and engaged that creativity of hers by making herb tinctures. She eventually sold her wares on eBay. Having extra time as well, Eve learned how to prepare organic preserves from their orchard's bounty. Delicious. She sold most of these to a local grocery shop in town! The two long-time lovers now had time to walk a lot, read a lot, cycle a bit, and talk about their thoughts on a variety of subjects that interested them. Eve realized her lifelong dream to paint. From computer engineer to art gallery owner to artist, she had always pursued pleasurable self-expression, but this had been her destination. She gave most of her paintings away; pleasing herself with creative, lasting, and inspiring gifts for family or friends. The neighbours thought more of them, however, and organized a small, well-received exhibition of her art at the local community hall.

Adam and Eve had found the Holy Grail: harmony within oneself, with the social surroundings, with their own "available piece of the universe" and with its everlasting foundation. Living in a currently driven society, they had quietly decided to go their own way, to do what was right *for them*. They had consciously chosen the path of moderation, a path open to everyone. Presently, they were able to assess their *actual* needs and to satisfy them through non-frantic, creative efforts, quite joyfully.

As their happiness gradually grew, so did their good health. Their two loving daughters progressed well at the university. The family bond grew even stronger than during their "high-flying" period. Adam and Eve also made a few close friends in the local community. They no longer felt alone against the world. Still, they felt they were somehow missing something. Adam knew what it was. Naturally, they discussed their thoughts now as well as their feelings and, together, made a consequential decision.

They wanted to meet their faraway "children." The orphans, who corresponded with them in ever-improving English, were about to graduate from their schools, dispersed all over the globe. It would be a gift for them, but also for Adam and Eve. Perhaps, it could be a special and useful gift for Rachel and Mary too. So Adam and Eve gathered the necessary sum and made the relevant arrangements. They decided to fly all ten children to their little paradise on five acres, and spend one month of the approaching summer with their young, exotic guests.

On a particularly beautiful day, they arrived. They put all the girls in the house with them, and the boys in two tents in the orchard. Amazingly, these young people of a roughly similar age, but from vastly different backgrounds, hit it off readily. They could all communicate in English without much trouble, and were each very curious about both the country they were visiting and each others' respective countries of origin. Predictably, Rachel and Mary did want to spend their vacation at home and get to know their "siblings." Again, they surprisingly clicked easily with their peers from far away. It looked as if this new generation, free of the immature complexes of superiority or inferiority displayed by previous generations, was able to relate naturally and evenly to one another. There was a lot of laughter and endless talk. The visitors were surprised at how frugally their "rich" benefactors lived. And it made them feel much more at home.

Adam and Eve were not only hosting the children, they were also trying to learn about them and from them, and they hoped to teach them something too. They showed them around the rolling countryside where they lived. They pointed out the acclaimed "pride of the county." It was a new, but already legendary, humongous super-mansion, known to boast fourteen bathrooms. None of the visitors were impressed. But they were surprised. At first, they talked amongst themselves. Then they giggled, and then openly laughed. Adam got his confirmation over the validity of his original hunch, or insight or whatever it was, that he'd experienced in that bygone Jacuzzi.

Perhaps it was in this context that the children, sitting one evening around a small campfire, asked Adam and Eve why they had one bathroom only and lived so modestly in comparison to so many others in their country? Before answering their poignant question, Adam asked them whether they knew who the Buddha was. Only Jaya, Sayed, and Bhopal knew. Adam explained to the others who Buddha was. Again, he asked them who knew about Jesus. Most of them knew Jesus. Adam rose and slowly added some wood to the fire. Then he said, "What I just did is that I created more light for you, so you could see yourselves, me, and what is around us with more clarity."

He continued, "These great teachers consciously added more light to the dying fire of proper human conduct and true knowledge. Each of them, with prudent care as well as love, left a beacon for humanity, a paradigm in both knowledge and conduct. Jesus condensed his paradigm, so it could be more easily remembered and applied. He said, 'Do unto to others what you would have them do unto you.' This single sentence, the Golden Rule, is a working definition of social accord. If consistently applied by individuals as well as nations, it could effectively—and relatively quickly, I might add—solve most of the problems humanity now faces. Buddha's beacon shined on the universal safety valve of moderation."

"The Golden Path," said Eve, realizing herself for the first time, the complementary teachings of Buddha and Jesus.

"That's right!" said Adam. "Buddha taught that the safest way to go, in every human life, is the 'the third way,' the special path between two extremes. That's the 'Golden Path.' To follow it, you have to think first, and detect the two opposite extremes in *possible future* proceedings as well, before making important decisions in the present. You want to try to prevent these extremes from occurring. Within them, danger and suffering inevitably await, as in an ambush—a predictable, preventable ambush. Somewhere between these, often spectacularly luring extremes, a safe passage is bound to open."

The kids listened in wide-eyed amazement. Were they following him?

"Okay, I'll answer your question more directly," said Adam. "Eve and I were young and inexperienced—even if bright and hardworking. Like so many others, we were lured by the one extreme of material possession.

We began developing the constantly modeled excessive need for physical comfort and false pride—those who have more … are *better*. At some point, though, we woke up. Fortunately. And saw that we had gotten trapped in an extreme."

This was news to the twins; Rachel spoke up, "How did you know?"

Eve didn't want her girls to feel like they were to blame, as kids often do, so she piped in. "You probably saw the signs in us yourself." She started to count on her fingers, "Anxiousness, emotional void."

"You mean when Dad would just sit and stare at the TV?" asked Mary. The other kids all giggled.

"Yes," said Adam, "You nailed me. I had this enveloping lack of deeper meaning—not that you girls and your mother weren't meaningful to me, of course you are—it's just that there is more to life than one person's tiny inner circle." He used his arms to show the difference between a close space near his body and a wider circle encompassing all fourteen of them. "So we broke out of our tiny social shell and looked around, on a global level. What we saw—" The memory of the impact of El Alto took his breath away. But by now, from the impact each of them had had on each of the others, everyone knew what he meant. He continued anyway, "Well, it confirmed for us the improbable scale of our extreme. So we decided to embark upon our moderate, golden path." The Greek philosopher Aristotle had defined it earlier as the Golden Mean

Eve thought Adam was sounding a little too proud—you can get ego-involved with your moderation too, she thought. "Of course, we are still very fortunate," she added and Adam nodded, urging her to go on. "We no longer have any even remotely unmanageable debts."

"Yes," he said, "we shed the extreme of being 'rich,' but have been very prudent and careful—"

"And lucky," interrupted Rachel, who knew they'd had a huge head start on all her new brothers and sisters. If her parents had taught her anything, it was never to be egotistical about your good fortune.

"And lucky," agreed Adam, "not to slide over into the other extreme of being poor. If we had, who would pay for the air tickets, and your education for that matter?"

Everyone laughed and Bhopal said, "That's so you can follow the Golden Rule, too, right?"

Yes, they understood the message perfectly. To seal the educational deal, Adam smiled and added: "I feel that I can comfortably look into the eyes of any poor person on our planet now, and say 'I am doing my part, are you doing yours?' Unless I am being criticized by an elderly or sick person, or by the hapless victim of a disaster, I can say—with all due respect, 'Maybe you could try a little bit harder; and please tell me specifically how I can help you do so.' And I promise all of you," said Adam, making eye contact with each orphan teenager, each of his own daughters, and his wife, "each of you, to do my honest best in this particular regard."

Although he'd purposely used his words quite bluntly, more laughter followed. This emotionally harder part of his message also very clearly came through.

With many lively conversations such as this, and a lot of fun, their genuinely interesting and rewarding days were passing much too fast. After a month, the time for saying goodbye arrived. In so little time, they felt like one family. Before parting, they all resolved to stay in touch and stand by each other in times of need. Mary and Rachel were already planning to visit each "sibling," or at least as many as they could, to learn about their societies firsthand. Someday, perhaps, they would return the favour. Adam and Eve were touched and promised their twins to help to the degree they could afford it. As for the athletic and intelligent positive-thinker, Ernesto, Adam made a resolution. He decided to finance the medical studies that Ernesto had long dreamt about, at the University of Sucre, an old Bolivian city renowned for its colonial architecture.

After an emotional departure, it seemed their small house in the fruit-laden orchard had become unbearably quiet. Initially, it felt sad. As they often did, Adam and Eve sat on the porch till late evening, sharing and discussing their feelings, thoughts, and observations in-depth. They agreed that they had accomplished something socially creative and important, despite their limited means. They had extended their family beyond geography, political systems, and religions. Also, they led by example in something useful, positive and—they hoped—lasting, for *twelve* younger others (for they included their own sweet girls), destined to live apart from each other. Moreover, just the two of them had managed to offer education and hope to ten who came from the anonymous masses of the most disadvantaged inhabitants of their blue planet and were now loved as their own children.

Adam suddenly noticed the first grey hair in Eve's long locks. He kissed that spot, and began caressing her delicate, freckled face with his strong, black-skinned hand. Eve's red hair looked like wavy flames lightly touched by a gentle breeze in the setting sun. Adam loved her face, radiating as it did with quiet intelligence, and also her red hair, endowed by her Jewish ancestors. Now, feigning innocence, she asked him: "Have you noticed that for some time I've tended to kiss the short curly hair I love so much in … well … just a few particular spots?" They both started laughing at the very same moment, understanding each other completely and, as always, enjoying a virtually identical sense of humour.

Honesty

Honesty could be compared
To cool and fresh water,
Offered free to anyone
That for a change begins longing
To cease a chronic thirst
And wash the dust-covered face,
With self-acceptance look
At now clean features in clear mirror

The steadfast commitment to honesty
For the brief pain of extracting
The lure of false gains
From one's too-driven mind
Assures that one will complete
One's lifelong quest for success
Attained with quiet dignity

Unlike the short-lived and unviable
Voided life of a trivial lie,
Honesty in practice does prove
That one could thrive not being afraid
And no more dependent
On routinely manipulating
Once desired, petty, and selfish outcomes

My grandfather, Dionysius, liked to talk to me now and then about the ways of the world. I was usually receptive—as much as a little boy could be. Once, he brought up the topic of honesty. His view was that despite appearances, it remained the best way to succeed in life. "How so, Grandpa?" I asked. My peers frequently lied. But back then, I did not know that the practice of lying went up, with a vengeance, to the very top of adult society. So he told me a true story, to which I listened with great interest. The story related to the Caucasus region, a mountainous area between Russia and Iran, and certain events that took place there at the dawn of the *twentieth* century.

Arguably, that region creates the toughest challenge on the planet to any imperial power with an appetite for a slice of seemingly-manageable more. Nowhere else have the small nations, societies, and colonies of interlocking clans presented such a unique and resilient mix of ancient traditions, sophisticated cultures, and endless tribal complexity. Also, possibly no other geographical area has demonstrated such a level of fierce and skilful resistance, superbly facilitated by the maze of its vast and rugged terrain. One particularly robust quagmire was entered into by the Russians. Comparing the United States' historically brief Wild West phase to Russia's long-term "Wild South" endeavour makes it appear downright relaxing.

Having graduated with honours from tsarist's reputable Kharkov Polytechnics, its newly minted engineer Dionysius accepted an assignment others carefully opted to avoid. For a handsome reimbursement, he became an engineer in the old Georgian city of Tbilisi, surrounded by the unforgiving, labyrinthine mountains in the heart of the Caucasus. The area was highly restless, marred with regular kidnappings for ransom and crafty ambushes for robbery, the land all carved up between local warlords from the perennially competing clans. The common denominator, however, was their hatred for the colonizing power from the north. The Russians, on profitable assignments there, rarely ventured beyond the city's perimeter, protected by its garrison. When they did, they would almost always use the *somewhat* safer main roads only.

In contrast, Dionysius felt like a fish out of water, if being just in the city. He was a highly intelligent, dynamic, personable, and unmarried young man, very curious about the interesting world around him. Lucky for him, he was not a colonial Russian by blood—a fact he certainly did not hide. Linguistically talented, he mastered the local language before long, and his genuinely friendly, honest, and respectful attitude; his culturally valued oratory skills; his interest in hunting; and his playfully artistic abilities, all soon made him a much sought after guest among the clans' chieftains in the green mountains. He was invited to lively festivities in remote villages where he sang with the locals, drank strong, homemade wine after improvising the required elaborate toasts, and could be persuaded to present his own specialty, playing the flute. He affirmed his hard-earned acceptance by mastering the highlanders' exceptionally challenging and fastest dance, the *Lezginka*, thought by the locals as impossible to be properly performed by any stranger.

His daily life was no fragrant rose garden, though. Dionysius got assigned, as the tsarist government's liaison engineer, to a hired team of experienced British engineers. They were supervising the joint project of an international cartel in conjunction with the tsarist government to build the five-hundred-mile-long pipeline for bringing oil over land from Baku on the Caspian Sea to the port of Batumi on the shores of the Black Sea. This obviously important project, realized in the forbidding terrain, was an enormous engineering challenge. The area also proved logistically very challenging to Russians due to local resistance or, at the very best a scornful lack of cooperation. Dionysius speedily fine-tuned his English, and advanced from a liaison to a sort of "junior" co-engineer, able to suggest to his more experienced and specialized colleagues, certain ad hoc creative solutions. He was a born inventor throughout his long and, indeed, colourful life.

The labourers had to be hired in neighbouring Persia, now Iran. They did not accept any currency except gold coins, which they consistently checked with their teeth, because, perhaps not unwisely, they did not trust any governments. At some point, the strategically important project came to virtual halt due to serious delays with pay. Understandably, the frustrated and angry Persians refused to work, threatening to leave if their wages did not come through. The delay was courtesy of a certain quasi-political warlord and highly devoted robber, Asad Aga, a local Robin Hood of sorts.

He suddenly declared that no Russians would be allowed through his remote fiefdom—characterized by rather fluid borders—and which happened to be the only passage to the fuming workers. Thus, he effectively blocked the delivery of their overdue payment. This situation became of grave concern to the helpless authorities in Tbilisi. Dionysius volunteered to solve the escalating problem creatively, and revealed his suggestion. The authorities thought that he had lost his mind, but in their growing desperation, they grudgingly accepted. After all, if the Tsar would get upset, they could end up in frosty Siberia really fast.

Dionysius resolved to deliver those four compact bags of gold roubles himself, refusing the offered army detachment. He invited only his personal assistant, to whom he honestly explained the risks involved. The man accepted. They left for the menacing mountains unarmed. Both were riding their horses, carrying basic supplies and two small bags of gold each. As foreseen, they were apprehended by the armed horsemen, tied up as prospect ransom, and brought to Asad Aga's camp. The first question he asked Dionysius in broken Russian was, "How did you even dare to go through my land alone, and with four bags of gold? Are you a madman?"

Dionysius answered him in a local language, "Everyone in Tbilisi knows about you, and I was told by many that you are an honest man, just fighting the invaders. I am not a Russian, I am a Pole. They invaded Poland as well. After hearing in the city what they said about you, I felt that I should talk to you, and you would accept my explanation. There are Muslims, like yourself, who have not been paid for their hard and good work. This is very dishonest, as well as unfair to them, but particularly to their families they must feed. I decided to hopefully amend that and came over to ask for your help. Please help me do the right thing."

Asad Aga answered, "Yes, they know me even in Tbilisi, and I am an honest man. Tomorrow I will give you my horsemen for protection, to make sure that the gold gets to the workers. You have come here unarmed, and you have been honest, and respectful of me. You are also brave. Tonight we will have a dinner, and you will be my guest of honour."

The festivities lasted all night. Dionysius surprised them all with his totally unexpected social prowess. He was singing along, reciting an old local poem about the bravery of the ancestors, or chewing with skilfully offered delight, as he'd been trained, the roasted lamb's eye, given to a guest of honour. After masterfully dancing the *Lezginka* to the frenzied music, he was applauded by the patriotic robbers, and Asad Aga went so far as to call him his friend. Accordingly, he sent the prettiest of his wives to Dionysius's tent for the night, so their friendship would be properly cemented. Here my grandfather suddenly stopped his fascinating story.

Being only eleven, I asked him eagerly, "What happened next, Grandpa? Why did she come? What did she do?"

Dionysius, still a handsome man even at the age of eighty-one, slightly smiled under his grey moustache. He just said, "It is time to learn some English," and he started to teach me one of his limericks, short verses, and such. But before the casual lesson, he asked me, "Did you see my point about honesty?"

I thought for a while and said, "Yes," as honesty clearly worked for my grandpa very well. On that particular evening, he chose to teach me one very short song, and made me learn it by heart. It started with "Twinkle, twinkle little star, how I wonder what you are, up above the world so high, twinkle, twinkle, all the night." Many years later I found that the original version did not seem to include the last three words. If so, my grandpa must have added them for some reason, known only to him.

His experiences from Caucasus met with a miniscule epilogue in my own life, about sixty-five years after he met with Asad Aga. As a student, I travelled through the same mystifying, enchanted green mountains and saw a small wooden mosque in a remote village. I tried to enter it, but an old villager in a large fur hat most angrily stopped me. I recalled Dionysius's story and, with a smile, politely bowed to the hostile local man. Then I told him in Russian the simple and honest truth. I said: "I am a Pole, and I have never been to a mosque. I just wanted to see it and praise Almighty inside. Please, help me to do it."

The old man broadly smiled back, showing surprisingly healthy teeth, and said incongruously, indeed, "Ah, Polish ... Madam Walewska ... Take off your shoes and come in, please."

Madam Walewska was the Polish mistress of Napoleon Bonaparte. *How on Earth would he know that?* I thought. Decades later, I accidentally learned that Poland produced, for some period, perfumes with that brand name. Still, how would such an aged, plain villager living up there in the remote Caucasus mountains know anything about Madam Walewska, whether the faded emperor's forgotten mistress or a positively obscure perfume? It is to remain his modest mystery.

Loyalty

Rare, for true to itself loyalty
Dwells in a sublime state of the fine mind,
Anchored in a core of heart,
And cannot be too easily offered
Simply to anyone ...

This uniquely fused state
Relies on a deeply intrinsic, lucid anticipation
Of feeling self-debased,
If not offering loyalty that is—itself
During trying hours
To the person chosen by that mind with heart,
Perhaps to the group,
Even to an abstract idea, embraced as worthy

Such a subtle, naturally sensed anticipation
Of that unbearable,
So impossible feeling,
Readily differentiates a truly loyal individual
From most others,
Those opting not to look into danger's sly eyes
Ultimately destined
To test the depth of loyalty best

This unique and true story was told to me by my grandfather, Dionysius, not
quite a year before he died, when I was fourteen and inquired about his late
wife, Anna, the grandmother I had never known. She passed away about two
years before I was born. I was all ears and, after hearing it, felt like I had met
her. Clearly, Anna's story belongs to the theme of loyalty.

   Both of Polish descent, they got married in old Tbilisi, nestled amongst
the enticing if dangerous Caucasus Mountains. Their promising lives—like
those of many others—were dramatically altered in 1914. All over Europe,
men were marching to local railway stations with enthusiasm proportional
to their maturity. Women, after bidding their emotional farewells, would be
facing along the new experience of chronic fear. Dionysius and Anna got lucky.
He was not, bewildered, boarding a crowded train towards the all-devouring
frontline. She was not, picturesque, left behind, waving a white handkerchief

in deepening sadness. Their train was destined for St. Petersburg, and she was legally accompanying him.

Dionysius was indeed drafted into the army, but his was a special assignment. An engineer with an excellent command of English, including technological terms, he had proven his effectiveness in working along with a large British organization. He was therefore deemed more useful far from the front. He reported to high military office as part of the technical negotiations with the British regarding the vital shipments of armaments via the northern port of Murmansk. The British were planning to send such aid to their embattled tsarist ally through there.

The couple settled in St. Petersburg and soon became part of the local high society. Life seemed not to be turning for the worse as yet. Dionysius was making friends in the otherwise fast-fading high places, while fulfilling his daily duties the best way he could. Not much had changed with the abolition of Tsar Nicolaus. Moreover, Dionysius personally knew Alexander Kerenski, who had assumed power of the Russian Provisional Government, and was a friend of the president of Russia's parliament or Duma, Rodzianko.

In the fall of 1917, their sheltered world changed rapidly. The Bolshevik coup hijacked the already advanced and largely peaceful revolution, sending it into its bloody phase. Lenin and his comrades established a centre of power in the Smolny Institute. After the collapse of any resemblance of social order, the often drunk bands of self-styled revolutionaries initiated their chaotic terror. They looted the wealthy, exerting their personal revenge for not having been wealthy themselves. Though ideologically inconsistent with their espoused views, wealthy would have been the more desirable state of affairs. It was not unlike the "Reign of Terror" displayed in France a few generations before or, for that matter, all the violent "property-aimed" revolutions before or since.

The "enemies of the people" became instantly defined as the "white-handed ones." The revolutionaries apprehended passers-by on the streets to check their hands. Those whose hands were not callused by long-term manual labour were taken into an improvised custody. Dionysius always worked hard, but mostly with his mind. After showing his hands, he was arrested on the spot. The "enemies of the people" were locally herded to a ground-floor apartment. They had to stand, about eighty of them—the apartment was not large enough to seat them all. The revolutionaries were in the yard, drinking by the bonfire and singing melodic, mostly melancholy songs, and now and then randomly whisking a man to be shot, after he naively pleaded for his life. Dionysius was sure that this would be his end too. He thought about Anna …

The next day, a small detachment of navy sailors, the only actually disciplined armed revolutionary force in St.Petersburg, sternly marched in.

They turned their bayonets against the frightened, self-styled revolutionaries, ordering them to surrender one prisoner. It was Dionysius. Now, bewildered and physically weak, he walked with his new captors through the blistery cold streets of the famous city, towards an unknown fate.

Anna had learned in horror from one of the neighbours that her husband had been arrested. She was told where the revolutionaries held their locally apprehended captives. Her inner voice alerted her to act quickly, if she were to save his life. In a sudden insight, Anna realized what she needed to do. She recalled the story Dionysius had told her about his student life at the Kharkov Polytechnics. He had had a friend, a student like himself, by the name of Leonid Krasin. They had shared a common interest in music and briefly rented an apartment together. Their ways parted, as highly idealistic and energetic Krasin became an even more devoted revolutionary, subsequently ending up in exile. Now back in Russia from England, he had just emerged in St.Petersburg as one of Lenin's closest co-workers, and was assisting him in organizing the Bolshevik government in the Smolny Institute. It was after Krasin that the largest of future Soviet icebreakers, including the first nuclear one, would be named.

Alone, she made her way through the dangerous streets of the lawless city to beg Krasin for her husband's life. Anna managed to sway suspicious security guards, and was eventually received by Krasin in his office. His response was as positive as rapid. He got Lenin's authorization to dispatch a small detachment of navy sailors from those who were guarding the Smolny Institute to bring Dionysius there. Loyal Anna had saved his life ... for the first time.

The two former students and now distant friends met after almost twenty years—presently under much different circumstances. Dionysius found Krasin as idealistic and devoted to his cause as ever. He was still living his passionate dream of revolutionary justice, social equality, and of—to be ultimately brought about by the revolution—happiness for all. At the end of their lengthy conversation, he offered his one-time friend nothing less than the post of Chief Commissar of the Putilovski Plant, a gigantic producer of arms under the tsarist regime. This sudden, strategic appointment had to be approved by Lenin. Krasin introduced Dionysius to him. During their short meeting, Lenin said, "The revolution needs good engineers and managers." He foresaw peace with Germany, but also widespread hunger in Russia. Accordingly, he told Dionysius to start converting the Putilovski Plant to the production of agricultural machinery instead of weaponry. (His plan may have also indicated that Lenin, so focused on making peace with Germany probably underestimated the scope of the unfolding Russian civil war, and did not foresee the parallel, lost war with Poland.)

This absolutely shocking appointment was sealed, giving Dionysius considerable power in the hungry city of St. Petersburg. Unbelievably, he now had at his daily disposal three thousand food staples (*pajok*), including the strongest vodka (*spirt*). It made his newly gained, "sweeping" power very real. At that extremely harsh time, only the luckiest of workers received such staples as pay. Alcohol was a priceless bonus. Within a few hours, he went from rags to riches and from imminent death to a secured life, albeit temporary. He perfectly knew that he did not belong there, but the extraordinary offer sounded a lot more attractive than a random shot by a groggy revolutionary at an unforgettable bonfire ….

Buying time, he lasted as a commissar for nearly two years. By then, the Soviet Union was fighting with the newly resurrected Poland … and losing—to the total if mostly pleasant surprise of Western powers—thwarting the planned export of revolution westward to an again restive Germany. Ruthless and obsessed with power, a young Joseph Stalin, who hated Krasin and the other educated and idealistic revolutionaries with a passion, skilfully began to fill the void created by a now gravely ill Lenin. Dionysius knew his days were numbered. After sharing his bold plan with Anna, he decided to shoot for the moon. He had a carefully prepared plan together with his equally carefully selected personal secretary, a former tsarist Pole, Colonel Pomaski. It would put their lives, as well as the lives of their agreeing, if frozen with fear, wives at a great risk.

When the two high-ranking armed "officers" from the *Cheka*, or "Extraordinary Commission," the first of a succession of Soviet security/intelligence organizations, dressed in their commissar leather coats and caps with red stars, accompanied by their female "comrade secretaries," produced their false documents at the railway station, they were immediately led to the train destined towards the Polish front. The revolutionary Cheka, being the father of the Soviet Union's NKWD and grandfather of the KGB, was unequivocally dreaded, and rightly so. A Cheka officer, if not cooperated with, could shoot anyone on the spot with effective impunity. Unsurprisingly, the officers were saluted and led to the designated compartment.

The first part of the escape plan had worked impeccably. The documents, bought with gold and diamonds, affected the authorities as expected, never mind the revolutionary upper-class's leather uniforms. According to the documents, the two Cheka officers had been dispatched to inspect the Soviet civilian authorities in the area close to the frontlines, bolster their morale the Cheka way, and generally assess the political sentiments of the local population.

At their destination, the alleged "Chekists" disembarked the train in order to, purportedly, embark on their worthy assignment. Instead, they changed their clothes, with relief. A local Byelorussian peasant agreed—for a large sum in gold roubles—to drive them through the porous frontlines to the Polish side … overnight, on sleds. He delivered, but not without some very tense, dangerous moments on the way.

In any case, they won their freedom and Dionysius reported to the Polish authorities. He and Anna started a new life once again. For the next twenty years, they lived happily in Warsaw where Dionysius—after some initial struggles—established a successful architectural and construction company. The Second World War would change everything in their stable lives again, as the former one had done.

The Polish government, in contrast to other governments in the region, refused to ally with Hitler. In the spring of 1939, Polish Intelligence loyally offered to surprised and grateful British and French expert envoys the basic decoding system of the "impenetrable" German military-code-machine, "Enigma," including the priceless actual machine! Cracked by Polish Intelligence mathematicians and later improved and expanded by the British, the ability of the allies to access the German code has been credited for shortening World War II by about two years. It prevented Hitler from developing his own atomic bomb on time …

On September 1, 1939, the Polish army was the first to oppose the Nazis militarily. It obviously lost, but it forced the invaders to take serious losses and to advance against it at the slowest pace, compared with later invasions across Europe. The battles lasted longer than Hitler anticipated. For example, young Polish Captain Wladyslaw Raginis commanding 720 soldiers managed to hold for 3 days on Wizna river the entire 3rd Army of Field Marshall Georg von Kuchner, equipped with 350 tanks and spearheaded by the Panzer Corps led by its famous commander General Heinz Guderian. The battle has been referred to as "Polish Thermopylae". That sacrifice, or perhaps contemporary, if largely unknown, gold standard of heroic loyalty and in-combat leadership allowed the main forces to regroup thus defend Warsaw longer. The loss of nearly seven hundred Nazi planes in the Polish campaign tangibly facilitated the critical Battle of Britain. Squadrons of Polish pilots effectively fought in that mighty battle.

The Polish infantry, among other actions, succeeded where various others consecutively did not. It finally broke the "invincible" German fortifications at Monte Cassino, opening for the allied forces the road to Rome. It was the special officer and envoy of Polish Resistance Jan Karski, who made it to the allied governments, begging with human loyalty for their action on behalf of the Jews exterminated in Nazi-occupied Europe. His astounding humanitarian action was described in the book "How One Man Tried to Stop the Holocaust" published in 1994. He was the first to inform the free world, in well-documented and shocking detail, about what was eventually named ... the Holocaust or Shoah. After the war, these facts, or examples of loyalty in action, were quite naturally "underreported" on both sides of the "iron curtain." The invasion by the Soviets on September 17, 1939, in a temporary alliance with Hitler, sealed the historically unlucky fate of this impeccably loyal ally, at the time still fighting in full formation.

The unforgiving Nazi occupation followed, and Dionysius, despite his age, joined the Polish Resistance. His risky assignment was to seek out German war profiteers. He recruited them among the engineers from the Todt organization, which technologically supported the German army mostly through transporting its weaponry. Every war has people who are always striving to get rich and loyal to no one but themselves. He took advantage of that proven, human phenomenon. Dionysius spoke workable German, but, more important, he had almost unlimited financial resources at his disposal. He was buying German light armaments from his recruited profiteers. Instead of reaching the front, they were ending up in Polish hands. Money for this and other operations similar to the ones Dionysius was involved in—British pounds and American dollars—was dropped for the Polish underground by parachute, together with other supplies. That money was marked. Certain British and American banks were printing subtly altered banknotes as part of the war effort.

However, after accompanying him for quite some time, Dionysius's good luck suddenly ended. One winter, two black Gestapo cars stopped at dawn in front of their apartment building. His wife, Anna, gravely ill at that time with cancer, heard the cars. Her inner voice once again told her that she had to act very fast. They had kept a large bundle of British pounds in a drawer. Anna quickly opened the window and put that bundle on a sill, covering it with wet snow that had fallen the night before. The Gestapo thoroughly searched their large apartment, but found nothing. They even opened the critical window, yet did not check under the snow. Nevertheless, Dionysius was arrested; someone must have reported him. His interrogation in the Gestapo headquarters, located on the infamous Szucha Street, was harsh. He was threatened and beaten, but still not tortured ... yet.

He knew nothing about anything, but obviously was not believed and predictably imprisoned. From that Pawiak prison, the Nazis would now and then escort a group of prisoners in cramped trucks to the Palmiry forest and summarily execute them in order to terrorize the defiant population. These group executions were conducted in an organized and orderly fashion—no melancholy songs, emotionally-charged behaviour, or drinking by a bonfire this time. The prisoners who avoided execution typically would be sent to perish in the concentration camps. Most loyally, ailing Anna went on her second major mission to save her husband's life. Frantically, with valiant resolve to battle her fast-growing physical weakness, she found the proper high-ranking Gestapo officer in time. For an unbelievably high bribe in pounds, that man was willing to release Dionysius. Through Anna, the requested amount was forwarded by the Underground. Soon after her husband's release, she passed away. Dionysius remained in hiding until the epic Warsaw uprising began.

He told me then, though I was such a young boy, that Anna was his relentlessly loyal and loving guardian angel throughout some thirty-seven years together. There must have been something to it … Through my own, quite robust commotions in life, I somehow have managed to salvage and preserve a glued-together cracked porcelain tile. An angel or goddess protecting a baby angel is painted in the glaze, submerged in what looks like a mythical aura or a realm of romantic melancholy. A prolific artist, it was Anna who painted that scene, the last artwork in her life and the only memorabilia I possess from her. Even in so volatile a time as those bygone years, some of those exquisite ladies apparently still cared about finely painting on porcelain—regardless.

Anna Poplawska {1879 - 1942}. Oil on porcelain.

Trust

The culinary-like art of investing trust,
Requires a pinch of creativity
And even more importantly—
A handful of well-seasoned pondering

The stark, much too far extreme,
Of never trusting anybody, just in case,
If utilized as a recipe
Would lead to a stigma, thus a social void

Then again gullibly trusting everybody
Is, most unfortunately,
One of the costliest, gravest mistakes,
Only sheer innocence can make

Yet the appeal of the extreme is so tempting,
Enticing to slide into,
As that, not uncomfortably,
Saves one from harder, critical thinking

Trust does work, as an adequate instrument,
When from the clear lenses of analysis
Its pursuer figures out
Who is trustworthy, and to what extent

An unconditional, steadfast trust,
Could be securely invested in the sea divine,
Even more so, if one
With sober realism well assists oneself

Eugenia's sunny character was, among other positive traits, gracefully expressed by her intelligent optimism. She very naturally trusted her life, so it gratefully reciprocated by offering her plenty of luck … given her circumstances. That luck, as any luck, at some pre-farewell point in her life simply ceased to exist. Not unlike a beautiful bird that inevitably and suddenly just … flies away.

Eugenia's trust, long rewarded by her faithful luck, had to work its way up from an extremely low baseline. She was not even three years old when the First World War broke out. As usual in Polish history, directly driven as it is by geography, the large foreign armies that were ordered to march towards the East had to advance through local soil, and those ordered to march towards the West, had to do the same. In one such movement, both of Eugenia's parents got collaterally damaged; that is, killed.

As much as Eugenia's age allowed for any conscious perception, she found herself cared for by someone in the evacuation train. It was not heading in the direction of the basked-in-the-sun Côte D'azur. That long train was slowly making its way to a very distant, frosty Siberia ... Even in that vast, ice-shackled, but also stunningly beautiful stern symbol of everyone knows what, somebody was taking care of her. Unlike some other evacuated children she did not die of hunger, disease, or the biting frost. She had a very rough early childhood, no doubt, but luckily she happened to have good local Russian people around. At the age of eight, much more conscious by now, she embarked on a ship carrying her to a new beginning. Surrounded by other children, Eugenia was again heading east. That particular ship had left the Russian port of Vladivostok for the Japanese port of Yokohama.

The First World War, as with any other war, after exhausting itself, inevitably ended in the more or less temporary peace. Some people of goodwill, backed by Poland's resurrected government and the International Red Cross, were anxiously rescuing the orphaned children of Polish descent from Siberia. The bloody revolution was about to reach there. They were to be brought home before it erupted. The ship of the budding wonder and hope of many orphans safely docked in Yokohama. Eugenia looked down from the deck in awe. She saw the delicate Japanese ladies in vibrant kimonos and their even more amazing colourful parasols. Those ladies constituted the charitable welcoming committee awaiting the orphans on the pier. After the grey and grim vegetation in Siberia, she trusted that she entered paradise.

The Japanese took care of the orphaned Polish children in an impeccable way. Some of them had to be hospitalized. The luckier ones just needed tender loving care. Everyone was nourished with healthy food and gentle touch. It almost started feeling like a home, even some initial friendships were made, but one day, the memorable and healing stay in Yokohama came to an emotional and tearful end. In her next sea journey, on the ship with a British crew, Eugenia traversed the long and roundabout route at first towards the south, then the west, the north, and again the east. The ship encountered a huge, lasting storm and the ship rode the powerful waves like a bronco. All the children were frightened, including Eugenia.

Somebody cried, "Where are we?"

Someone answered, "On the Indian Ocean!"

Eventually the ship came to the port of Gdansk, Poland, on the Baltic

Sea. Close beside that old city, the new port of Gdynia was being built where the Polish government established school with a dormitory for the orphaned "Siberian children," brought back from peril. They were well taken care of in their new place. Indeed, so far Eugenia had always felt taken care of, despite her social handicap. Even having lost her parents, she grew up feeling that she could trust her life, her fate, and those around her.

Upon completion of their primary education, the more academically promising children underwent an exam. The successful ones were to be sent to the capital city of Warsaw where the government had organized a School of Commerce specifically for them. Again, Eugenia trusted her life and was not disappointed. Not only was she sent to Warsaw, but in time caught the loving eye of a certain wealthy lady by the name of ... Anna. She was working as a volunteer in the dormitory with the orphans, teaching them general arts and painting on porcelain. There were many fine girls in the school, but she took a special liking to beautiful Eugenia, who radiated respect, grace, and trust. Eventually, Anna invited Eugenia home.

After several years Anna became her mother-in-law. Their very-good-catch son fell in love at first sight meeting Eugenia in his parents' place. So did Eugenia. He could not imagine his life without marrying the once pitifully abandoned, now educated, smart, and particularly charming young woman. His well-established family recognized the staggering financial disparity, but as they had already fallen in love with Eugenia, too, decided it didn't matter. However, not everyone in their upper class agreed, branding the couple a spectacular misalliance. Indeed, her only dowry—which proved to be sufficient—was the treasure of her hard work at school, her personal glamour, optimistic trust, high intelligence, and last but certainly not least, her graceful beauty.

After graduating from the Lvov Polytechnics, Eugenia's practical and energetic husband established a successful engineering company. The years to come evolved to be a happy peak in her previously so challenging life. Now, she was a young and much-loved-by-her-husband lady. She was living in an elegant European city, in a nice suburban villa with a large garden. Eugenia liked her work and was so fond of driving her own car to the bank ... She has decided to keep her job. It all seemed to be too good to be true ...

After several years the chronic tumour of the collective human psyche manifested itself again; this time in the form of the Second World War. By the end of it, Eugenia had become a widowed, destitute refugee, fighting for the survival of herself and her two little children. No one close to Eugenia who had survived had means to help her. Her remaining years were marked by uphill economic struggles hampered by seriously deteriorating health. In spite of it all, she tried to continue with her trust and sunny optimism that things would change for the better. But they did not—at that time.

She routinely found herself trembling in an unsheltered streetcar stop, while waiting on windy, frosty mornings for a ride to her pittance-paying clerical job. Eugenia wore a thin autumn coat only, waiting for that streetcar that seemed to never come. In sad truth, she simply did not have enough money to buy a proper winter coat. Her pursuit of some odd, additional clerical jobs still was not sufficient to save enough, given other relentlessly unfolding emergencies. Rather, her efforts seemed to sap the rest of her gradually diminishing energy. After a long battle, cascading down from bad cold, to pneumonia, to asthma, to a coronary disease, she began disappearing in a slew of hospitals for increasingly longer periods of time. Subsequently, at the age of forty-seven she passed away.

Before she did, Eugenia called to the hospital bedside her fourteen-year-old son, Victor. With the bravely attempted shade of a smile she said, "I am asking you to give me your word that you will do something very important for me. I deeply trust that once you give me this word, you will keep it. Now promise me that regardless of what, you will always continue with your schooling." Her son agreed before their profound farewell. His task would be a challenge indeed, in particular given her caveat, "regardless of what."

Eugenia's natural trust, expressed at the time she was preparing to depart was validated, proving her vision of reality was true. After all, would she have ever even gotten out of Siberia if she had not embraced, with trust, the goodwill and warmth of strangers? Or, perhaps more accurately, trusting the sublime Goodwill in the mysterious wisdom behind all human beings' bafflingly diversified fate?

Courage

—In memory of Irena Sendler

The strongest man is he who stands alone in the world.

—Henrik Ibsen

Even renowned integrity surely needs its best bodyguard
By simple name of … firm courage

Without that focused, hard trained, always battle-ready trait,
The glory of integrity sooner rather than later
Would fall into self-compromise

To integrity, the one disgraced well,
The most important from all doors would not open invitingly

Now it has to wait for long, shaking out naked in the cold,
Until appropriately humbled,
It reconciles with once dismissed, albeit indispensable friend

For neither the too-meek-goodness holds the fitting key
Nor does intention have it,
And never has it cowardice, hidden behind a mask of realism …

A war may remind one of the enormous test invariably defining who actually is … who. It can bring forth the worst in those unfortunate to face it, but also … the best. A total war creates the utmost challenge in such test. Its toughest part could be a precisely organized cold-blooded, massive genocide, disguised as combating the enemy during a war. Yet, the war mega-crime of this scope always fosters a decision in certain individuals to stand up and confront the oppressors for the sake of exterminated others. Even to fight alone, if required. There has never been a more relevant test for humanity, than the sub-barbaric abyss of the Holocaust.

The most challenging difficulty in this test emerged in Eastern Europe. For example in the Nazi-occupied Poland, unlike anywhere to the west, for sheltering or even briefly helping a Jew, an altruistic culprit would be "by law" shot on the spot, together with his or her immediate family. In spite of this, the names bestowed by the Yad Vashem Institute in Israel with the honour, "the Righteous among the Nations," for having the courage to save Jewish lives in the Nazi-occupied parts of Europe, are massively Polish.

Indeed, there is no better example of courage than one shown by those who declare a personal war against a vicious, armed-to-its-teeth, totalitarian might to take back from the powerful enemy's claws as many innocent lives as possible. Accomplishing that utterly difficult goal is more important to such special persons than their own lives.

Examples of these unique human beings include: Raul Wallenberg, a Swedish diplomat in Nazi-occupied Budapest, Hungary, managed to peacefully save thousands of Jews. As did, though on a lesser scale, the German businessman, Albert Schindler, portrayed in Stephen Spielberg's film *Schindler's List*. A not well-known German soldier, Otto Schimek, flatly refused to carry out Hitler's order to exterminate Jews. With quiet bravery, he faced the inevitable consequences. A Polish nurse, Irena Sendler, was recently recognized worldwide, just before her death, for saving about 2,500 Jewish children from the Warsaw Ghetto right under the nose of the Nazis. A young Polish Jew, Mordechai Anielewicz, spearheaded the Jewish armed self-defence in Europe, co-organizing, and then commanding, the Warsaw Ghetto uprising in the spring of 1943. Except for Schindler and Sendler, they all paid with their lives.

These individuals could be compared to the shining tip of a remarkable iceberg, with its main silent mass submerged under the surface of our knowledge and memory. The submerged mass of courage and altruism consisted of very many others. They were, like unknown soldiers, "the *Unknown* Righteous among the Nations," less stunning, less effective, but identically motivated and courageous, if obscure. I offer you two such examples.

The first of these two individuals I personally and closely knew, until his death in 1990. A Polish engineer, Kazimierz Klinowski, was a manager of a brick factory during the war, close to the labour/concentration camp in Plaszow on the outskirts of Krakow. This particular camp, with its hateful and unpredictable SS commander Ammon Goetz, was factually depicted in the movie, *Schindler's List*. Kazimierz spoke perfect German with no accent, as he grew up and was professionally trained on former German territory. That factory ultimately operated under Nazis supervision. Kazimierz made all possible efforts to persuade the Nazis to assign him Jewish workers from the nearby camp. Due to his perseverance and impeccable command of German, he was successful.

He would, as often as he could, feed the hungry and exhausted Jews and let them lie down inside that small factory during a part of a shift. The Polish crew worked harder and longer so the Jews could have a bit of reprieve from their ordeal under Goetz. He also, most illegally, employed as a clerk a Jewish acquaintance by the name of Jakubowicz. He ran into him, now a hungry fugitive on the street, and took him in, protecting him and arranging false documents for him. Klinowski worked for the fugitive's father before the war as a manager in a brick factory in the town of Mikolow. The offered help was given under the condition that Jakubowicz never revealed their connection if something went wrong. Much later, spotted during a Nazi snap-inspection of that factory and apprehended by the Gestapo, Jakubowicz kept his promise until his death, never betraying his benefactor.

Being drawn to work in Klinowski's factory became something of a modest blessing for many victims. He was doing what he could to save lives, risking his own. He was interrogated on three occasions and threatened by the Gestapo—and once by Goetz himself, who grew suspicious, possibly after a phone call from the Gestapo, regarding Klinowski's rationale for more and more Jewish workers. This psychopath in a black uniform was known to kill in anger …

The war was coming to its end. The steadfast Polish ally had traded an orderly but lethal occupation for a chaotic, gradually debilitating, but non-lethal one. Right after the "liberation" by the Soviets, Klinowski saw from his window two approaching armed Jewish militiamen. They wore red stripes on their sleeves, an obvious sign that they had joined the new, Soviet-sponsored regime. He was sure that they were coming to shoot him, mistaking him for a Nazi collaborator, so he said a last goodbye to his wife. Instead, they were coming to thank him on behalf of the, almost annihilated, local Jewish community for protecting their oppressed brothers and to express their personal respect and gratitude.

I heard Kazimierz talk about those dramatic events *en passant*, very casually during supper, as our conversation focused for a while on the past occupation. He most genuinely did not think that what he did was in any way extraordinary. Being praised, he said, "Come on, *it was not a big deal*, any normal person would have done the same thing in my place." On the contrary, in my estimation *the deal was huge.*

The second example pertains to a lieutenant of the Home Army—the Polish Resistance—whom I never met. This information came to me directly from his wife and father. The lieutenant, fighting as part of the special-ops forces, *Kedyw*, was given orders in 1942 to open a metal shop, ostensibly producing pans, pots, mugs, and such. In the cellar, he was to run a top-secret clandestine operation. In that cramped space, several fighters working long hours were manufacturing hand grenades.

In April 1943, the Warsaw ghetto began to fight against the Nazi exterminators. It soon became inflamed, as the SS took unexpected losses and proceeded to quell the desperate uprising house by house. The surviving Jews were rounded up in groups of varying sizes and escorted out of ghetto to the infamous *Umschlagplatz*. There they were forced to board trains that were destined for gas chambers, disguised as large baths, which the Nazis operated round the clock in designated concentration camps.

The cookware shop was situated close to the burning ghetto's walls, so the street was, at times, filled with black smoke blown by the gusting winds. The lieutenant would stand in the doorway and, with mounting anger, watch exhausted civilians and some fighters being escorted to their deaths. In one particular moment, a thicker screen of smoke than usual billowed down and the next large group limped on. Seizing the opportunity, the lieutenant jumped forward and grabbed the two nearest men. He pulled them to his shop and immediately hid them under the counter. Luckily the loosely scattered troops did not notice anything because of the smoke and because the chaotically formed groups had not yet been counted.

The rescued Jews were fed and kept in the cellar for two days, before the notified superior officer came over. Both men wanted to fight the Nazis, and so were sworn in as new soldiers of the Home Army. They were transferred overnight to a partisan camp in Kampinos forest near Warsaw. The lieutenant's family never heard what became of them. When the lieutenant's wife told me this story on two occasions, she still had a look of mortal fear in her eyes. Had the SS noticed, her husband would have been instantly killed. She would have died at the hands of the Gestapo later. Soon after the event, she asked him why he did it. His answer was simple, "*I just had to.*"

The lieutenant's father gave me yet another perspective on the topic, as a second colonel in the same battalion. His son was highly commended by his superiors for bravery. However, in the same breath, he got a stern reprimand for jeopardizing the entire operation, the lives of his soldiers in the cellar, and potentially the lives of many others. If caught alive, everyone would have been tortured. Under such circumstances, regardless of how brave, sooner or later, names would have been divulged. I was deeply intrigued and asked both of them what happened to that lieutenant afterwards.

Some fifteen months later, the equally doomed, tragic epic of the Warsaw uprising erupted. The main Nazi forces sealed the district held by the Old City's defenders still fighting, but surrounded by the two SS brigades. One, SS Sonderbrigade Dirlewanger, commanded by the known degenerate SS *brigadenfuehrer*, O. Dirlewanger, a psychopath and alcoholic, was exclusively comprised of convicted German criminals, most with major offences. The perhaps fitting other, SS Sturmbrigade RONA, was led by the ex-Soviet renegade general, B. Kaminski. It was largely formed by the ex-Soviet POWs captured earlier by the German army who, some maybe reluctantly, volunteered to the SS and were already highly proficient in certain "special tasks." Interestingly, after the uprising ended, Kaminski was executed by the regular German army for his cruelty towards civilians. Dirlewanger was executed immediately after the war by the allies. Our resistance lieutenant fought in the defence of the nearly constantly bombarded Old City, surrounded by these two joint forces.

The only path of escape for about five thousand civilians caught up in the battle was the city's sewer system. Otherwise, they would be captured, raped, and murdered. There were a few precious openings to those Old City sewers, still in Polish hands. These openings had to be defended at any cost, so the civilians, the wounded, and then as many fighters as possible could evacuate. The lieutenant decided to stay put along with those troops determined to stop the advancing SS. The outgunned defenders held the line for as long as they could and succeeded in evacuating thousands of civilians and wounded before being overwhelmed.

Our lieutenant never returned from the vast graveyard of stark ruins. Awarded the Cross of Valour by the Poland Home Army, the decoration did not reach him on time. He shared his fate with other Warsaw fighters, including the Jews fighting in the ghetto and the gentiles, fighting throughout the entire city a year later. The winter was particularly harsh. The smouldering skeletons of houses were covered with a thick bandage of soft snow, falling on what once was a vibrant European capital. It also, mercifully, covered bodies of all the fallen, regardless of who fought whom or why. Their bewildered souls, facing sudden liberation, had already left the battle.

The lieutenant's second-colonel father, a born survivor, decided not to surrender with the others. He knew what captivity would be like. Although his neck had received minor wounds from a sniper, he made it through the dangerous, eerie ruins alone. Then he jumped onto a slow commercial train on the outskirts of the former city, to start a new life elsewhere, though he didn't know where. After all, he was only sixty-seven years old.

The second-colonel's name was Dionysius, my grandfather, and the lieutenant, his only son, was named Witold. He was my father, and his widow was Eugenia, my mother. After passing a transit-concentration camp in Pruszkow, she brought me into the still-warring world exactly three months after her husband was killed in action, and named me after him. Both Dionysius and Eugenia passed away not too long after telling me in detail the true story of my father, who had felt so abstract to me. I was thirteen.

Lieutenant Witold Poplawski's story speaks for itself. He was a man of significant courage. His genuine need to protect the jeopardized lives of others overrode any fear he might have felt. It is possible Irena Sendler, Raul Wallenberg, Albert Schindler, Mordechai Anielewicz, and Otto Schimek would not have rejected the company of Kazimierz and Witold. Or the company of the many others like them, irrespective of how modest their lives were or how obscure their stories are bound to remain.

Humour

Wild Mother Nature likes to beautify, with fresh flowers,
Her wavy hair in all shades of green,
Hoping to sway the overwhelming immensity of existence ...

Similarly people like accenting a hard life with humour
To at least briefly act as if,
To pretend an independence from their set circumstances,
Thus, in spite, establish with new hope
The joyful safety niches for relaxed, if short, well-being

The intuitive types may develop an elaborate coping skill
Shown as a good sense of humour,
Then laugh their shrewd way through the midst of it all ...

They naturally prove to be right, and longer live in health,
If heeding their humour's fine line,
Since the stealth thread of tragedy stays woven into a life
And black-marks the unmindful,
Those giggling at funerals of people, or dear to them ideas

Among nature rid of flowers, the empty life without humour
Could too early entice the end time
Of dry, icy winds, aimlessly swirling among lifeless craters ...

There exists an endless spectrum of the everyday sense of humour shown by
very common people. If they happen to face a degree of long-term potential
danger, their humour tends to evolve into two related branches. One is
"gallows," another, the "condensed-pure-nonsense." There could be at times
a mix of the two. The essence of this coping mechanism hinges on verbally
reducing certain dimensions of reality to sheer nonsense. It somehow absorbs
the perceived or anticipated danger, converting it to a sort of nonsense too, if
not almost a laughable matter. This story touches on that somewhat "crazy"
type of humour.

Young and fit as two fiddles, Victor felt compelled to explore the two
extremes of his character equally—his distinctly curious and independent
mind, and his incongruently muscular body. The first was his early and
consistent attempt to study the illuminated minds of humanity. This

required reading comparatively analyzed religious texts, various philosophical systems, and the classics. Which he did—voraciously, persistently, thinking and rethinking again.

The second pole meant taking on the most strenuous manual labour he could find, preferably in severe conditions. His brief formal encounter with weight lifting was over. Victor could not satisfy himself with exerting a serious physical effort without some directly useful, lasting, and practical results. For example, erecting a new concrete post, building a stone retaining wall, or unloading a large pile of sand from a freight train to make cement blocks would qualify. Having worked as a labourer in varied, physically challenging settings *on the surface* of Earth, he now resolved to fulfill that particular need *below* ground, raising a few eyebrows in the process.

He would become a miner. Sure enough, on one early morning, Victor found himself in a large, faintly rusty basket lift, slowly making its way into the darkness below. The metal basket creaked downward seemingly forever, as Victor watched the wet walls of the narrow shaft here and there dotted with dim lamps. Would the lift never stop? Would the tarnished basket eventually crash through the thin eggshell of the lithosphere and burst upon the enormous, barely contained inferno inside? A cold shiver passed his shoulders.

The other men in the lift did not seem to entertain such lofty associations. Instead, their lively conversation was simply a string of punctuations, swearing generously at semantically proper junctions. They were talking and laughing in a choir. Victor began to focus on them instead of following his futile thoughts. He quickly realized the men observed certain rituals. The miners of all different ages aptly competed in shocking each comparing the intensity and duration of last night's alleged exploits with their "old ladies." They knew damned well that they were lying through their teeth, but that seemed to be the very point. The older and more depleted a man ludicrously bragging about his fabulous prowess and the madly satisfied responses of his particular old lady, the louder the laughter erupting in the lift. They continued to descend through the darkness to the depth of half a mile over the scratched helmets with the attached small lamps worn by the laughing men. Hearing the next "I swear she almost fainted when I again ..." boasted by the aged short miner, Victor could not help it and fell into laughing with them. The laughter provided the illusion of safety on the floor of the dark corridor and the small open carts of the underground train.

Shelves were hung in regular intervals along the walls, piled high with a greyish powder. Victor asked the man beside him what it was. "Stone dust," he answered. Its purpose was to block the spread of a methane blast, which the coal mine was prone to, a simple but useful Polish invention. A methane explosion was certainly no laughing matter, but the miner began laughing as he looked at Victor's facial expression. Surely, laughter was a custom on this new job, even if not part of the job description.

The next few challenging days were no laughing matter either. Together with other new workers, Victor carried heavy steel elements and even heavier wet wooden poles along the dark, narrow corridors, sometimes not high enough to stand in. The tired rookies did not joke or laugh. The invisible weight of the half-mile above seemed to take an emotional toll too. Already labour-hardened Victor was soon tapped by a team of better paid, experienced miners looking for a new hand. Now he was working as a loader. After a senior miner had blasted a coal wall with dynamite, Victor would shovel his piles of coal to a long metal transponder, which would be moved a bit overnight for the next day's shift. Its deafening motor inched it along, running non-stop along the uneven, black wall. Having completed some seven hours of shovelling, he still had to work. In his best interest, he would build up the heavy wooden poles supporting the newly created ceiling above him. That was his daily, very strenuous merry-go-round. Although the loaders and senior miners were at times separated in the mines, working in different areas, Victor noticed another ritual that invoked some pretty crispy manifestations of "trench humour."

The miners were on lunch break. Munching on the simple lunch packets prepared by their no-doubt grateful "old ladies," they left their previous hot topic alone. The old ladies apparently belonged only to the "basket phase" of the day. At lunch, they exchanged either dirty jokes or jokes about dirty politics. Each joke, in direct proportion to its perceived quality, triggered a salvo of loud, echoing laughter. Their dirty jokes were similar to dirty jokes heard everywhere people in the world like to tell them.

The political ones were pretty indigenous though, like this one: "Kennedy meets with Khrushchev. Each of them tries to convince the other about the superiority of their own army with better soldiers. To prove their points they agree on conducting a three-pronged, practical test. The first step is to make it on time through the mock frontline. They randomly select one American and one Soviet grunt. Both passed with speed and valour. The second step was to shake the paw of a mother bear in the woods, and the third, to seduce a very hard-to-get pretty woman. The American soldier went to the forest but did not return. The Soviet returned from the woods after a long time, all bruised, bitten, and scratched. Then he saluted and reported, "Comrade first secretary, I did meet my objective! Let's now get this test finished. Where is that pretty woman I am supposed to shake hands with?"

Such compensating, less than intellectual—or to put it better, stupid— jokes appeared to be a well-established part of this hard life down below.

Their presence was as creative and predictable, as was their hearty laughter. But on one shift, the coal mine itself reminded everyone that a shield of laughter does not necessarily guarantee safety.

A large, heavy wooden pole suddenly slipped from a transmission belt, killing a young miner. There were no jokes that day, no laughter, just gloom. The same went for the second day and the third. On the fourth day, as the miners slowly descended in the lift, a wizened old miner mentioned something about his old lady, who, as he duly reported, had lately become ever so needy. The lively conversation took off, and the laughter gradually returned. The period of mourning was over. Indeed, a sense of humour often helps people in potentially menacing, as well as monotonous and isolated circumstances.

Perhaps a fitting example here could be the authentic song that the Roman legionnaires sang on their return from the danger-ridden victorious campaign against the barbarians. At that time, the important—in fact ultimately vital for any aging civilization—role of barbarian was played by the Germanic and Anglo-Saxon tribes. The legions' supreme leader, revered by his army, was the illustrious Julius Caesar, known to be not an overly hairy type. The plainly affectionate song roared by legionnaires, included the following lyrics: *We drag with us home this bald f***r! Hey Romans, keep your wives locked up well* ... The military's contemporary, open-ended couplets, starting with the "I don't know, but I was told ..." while somewhat less potent, seem also to be a bit more politically correct.

The epilogue to this story, though, touches on abstract humour, one with a little droplet of nostalgia. This epilogue deals with Victor's larger-than-life grandfather, Dionysius. After fighting in Warsaw's ground zero and leaving the mortally wounded and the yet-to-be-rebuilt city for good, he settled down in the coal mining region of Silesia. Again an engineer working in a foundry, he continued with his lifelong passion to invent new technology and improvements on old technology. He figured out a device—yet another simple but useful Polish invention for the miners—which the authorities eventually introduced in the local coal mines' baths.

Instead of miners keeping their clean personal clothes and their dirty work clothes in the same locker, the miners would keep them separate now. Not unlike lifting a flag on a mast, they would lift their clean clothing and other property to the high ceiling on an attached chain with a few hooks. Then they would lock that chain with a small personal knob connecting two rings. After the shift ended, they would unlock the knob, pull their property down, and lift the work clothing up same way. It was a less expensive, more hygienic, and more secure solution, saving some space too.

Now impoverished by the war, but still keenly creative, Dionysius did not receive his expected monetary reward for this invention. Instead, the engineer was honoured with a sizeable, colourful diploma. The certificate pictured a trinity of the profiles of Marx, Lenin, and Stalin, with their affable rosy cheeks and their sacrosanct facial hair, gazing into the bright future above a tacky spray of red roses. For quite some time, Dionysius was the laughingstock of his colleagues, despite his respectable age and experience. They promptly paraphrased the popular Polish saying, "succeeded like Zablocki on soap," to "succeeds like Dionysius on baths."

To explain, Zablocki was a seventeenth-century nobleman who decided to make quick money through commerce. He invested in a large amount of soap for exporting. To avoid an export tariff, he attached his heavy load of soap under rafts with ropes, with the idea of smuggling the goods down the Vistula River to the port of Gdansk. Alas, in his zeal, he did not foresee that the water would wash away his product. Hence, the axiom, "succeeded like Zablocki on soap," in other words, *a fool and his money are soon parted*. As the era of the ethnic joke has fortunately become passé, including the persistent *Polish* ones, this treasure hidden in the Polish language can now be reasonably shared!

Returning to Dionysius … Before he presented the prototype, he had invested some money and quite a lot of spare time in his own project. Unfortunately, like Zablocki, he did not foresee the inevitable consequences of his creativity. However, it wasn't the collegial teasing that caused Dionysius to exhibit his pretentious plaque above the white throne of his small bathroom.

Years after, standing in such a clothes storage area leading to his mine's bath and using the same diploma-consecrated chain-device himself, Victor saw the situation as ironic *and* abstract, hence hilarious. He pulled the chain and laughed. The similarly black-dust-covered miners looked at him with suspicion. After all, there was no reason to laugh anymore, let alone to oneself—all the miners were safe, up on the surface of their not-too-funny part of the planet. Strangely enough, no one mentioned a word about anybody's old lady passionately awaiting her ever-invincible and youthful old man although it was time to go home.

Make yourself all simplicity.

—Marcus Aurelius

Simplicity

The gift of innocent simplicity
Has been offered justly
To every living creature
Except for the still trapped
Between the animal and the divine
The self-beleaguering
Challenged human mind

That well stimulating challenge
Calls for a discovery
Of an agreeable method
For converting the presence's
Simplistic artificial complexity
Towards the future's
Complex natural simplicity

Helpfully to us, challenged,
Those trail-blazing the upper skies
Enigmatic far-stars' minds,
Through the messengers said
That the noblest knowledge-tree
For our in-blue garden,
Grows in simplicity of clear heart

Highly intelligent and sensitive, Marcel had been a creative, promising student even in his exquisite high school situated in Fontainbleau, France. It was after entering the seasoned Sorbonne University, however, that he discovered—soon to consume him—his emerging desire to write poetry. He began a prudent study of the poetry of unequivocally modern poets only. The stale rhythms and worse rhymes of outdated genres did not appeal to him. More important, no recognized poet wrote that way anymore.

He tried his best to understand their ultra-modern texts. Despite Marcel's quite analytical mind, he by and large had not been able to do so, at least to his satisfaction. Clearly, the subtle art of the most modern poetry must have been about something else, something above common, mundane understanding. Was it about feelings then? Marcel had made sincere efforts to explore his own feelings, while perusing the locally acclaimed chapbook poetry. With some exceptions, this poetry simply did not elicit any particular, let alone memorable, feelings in him. Thus, through elimination, he ruled out the domains of understanding and feelings as the cornerstones of this radically modern poetry.

Then what was that genre, trying to cut its own elusive edge, all about? Was it just literary yearning for a pure and abstract aesthetic? Unfortunately, the majority of texts Marcel perused did not bring him any really positive aesthetic experience. Sometimes quite to the contrary. No doubt, the ultra-modern poetry he studied was not about aesthetics. He broadened his search to realize, surprised, that only a miniscule number of readers seek this type of poetry. It looked as though there would not be any reward in it. He assumed that they were not grasping, as he now had, that this genre of poetry does not aim to facilitate understanding, foster memorable feelings, or satisfy the need for aesthetics. There seemed to be no convincing explanation for this massive omission phenomenon other than the fact that, regrettably, readers were not astute enough to grasp and digest the extra-modern poetry. Or, to climb the too steep and winding path that leads nevertheless to the shiny peak of its clouded Parnassus.

Puzzled, Marcel resolved to read through those thin volumes again, carefully enough to allow time for hindsight to kick in. Increasingly interested and absorbed, he started discovering an enticing, cognitive thread across these hermetic works. His exploration revealed that the art of the most modern poetry was about *words*, first of all, and less about the meaning they might or might not make to any potential reader, even intelligent and adequately educated. It seemed not to be about readers in general. If they existed in the poet's mind at all, it was on the periphery, almost as passers-by of the artistic process. What was that sublime, word-centered process all about?

The poems focused on connecting words in a striking way and clustering them into baffling, complex configurations, striving for the effect of a bold and cognitively menacing "literary frontier." Frequently, to the point of bravely defying conventional semantic properties. Marcel found this fine, intellectual and increasingly attractive, game indeed fascinating! Interestingly, the bolder and more complex these artistic thrusts were, the more the poem received, even if just locally, critical acclaim.

Only the very best among these modern poets were successful in getting their generation's fresh, creative perspective on paper and out to some segment of reality. Their remaining cohorts were just treading their complex, and tight sealed against any spillage, if muse-bestowed liquid. Perhaps they were more like hard-working prospectors, devotedly panning out water mixed with gravel, mostly with no success of turning up even one recognizable gold nugget in their artistic pans—as far as readers could be concerned anyway.

Marcel concluded that even if such modern poetry was not about reader response, it was still very much about the realm of human *affect*. Namely, the intense emotional life of the poets themselves. Remaining for him to find out was whether the writing was simply a vehicle for poets to vent their undercurrent feelings, in hopes of an emotional cleansing or catharsis? That made him wonder: would a catharsis-based literary process strengthen or weaken their artistic expression? In general, he wanted to know, why did they write? And what was it that they desired to say to the hypothetical reader?

Perplexed, Marcel honestly asked himself, what was it that he wanted to convey to readers as an aspiring poet? Would he be able to, even modestly, contribute to their lives through his art? These were good questions, but he did not have the answers. Maybe he had nothing of substance or recognizable value to offer potential readers. Still, he felt highly motivated and knew he was capable of consistently and joyfully working with words! Also true enough, he did have certain emotions that bothered him if left unarticulated. Ultimately, the ambitious, intelligent, and creative young man wanted to become an acclaimed poet.

Marcel enthusiastically embarked upon his artistic training. He advanced it in various inspiring Parisian Montparnasse cafés over time, like many artists did before him. He wrote cognitively complex, configurations of words striking original associations that were deft, shocking, fresh, and abstract. Eventually they received the recognition of some of his published peers. Step by step, he was becoming a poet noticed by local critics as well as a small circle of literary colleagues. Even without having too much to say to the potential reader, he eventually gained a few hundred readers in his country, renowned for its culture. Over the years, he made a decent enough living as a professor of literature in Touluse, and became the acclaimed master of his beloved avant-garde poetry. Accomplished in his craft, his poems were very imaginative, if not too meaningful, and indeed cognitively challenging, if cathartic only to himself.

Delicate Yoshi, a painter, had never made a name for herself, even though striving for perfection was in her first, second, and third natures. At the beginning of her career, she embraced photo-realism as her style. Her paintings were so meticulous they could be mistaken for high-resolution photographs. She eagerly painted what she saw with her gently precise eyes. Yoshi always made every effort to depict her carefully chosen theme in all its minute complexity: a portrait of a lady assembling flowers in the *ikebana* style, a scene with crowds of demonstrators waving colourful banners on the street, or a still life set up in her small and thrifty studio.

On one uneventful spring day, it occurred to her, that others probably did not need her realistic pictures—they could get the same scene with a camera. She stopped painting. She ceased attending social activities. She went into seclusion, where her perfectionist nature as an artist began, in healing silence, reinventing itself.

To the surprise of her bohemian friends, she returned to the art community as an abstract painter, equally devoted to the ideal of perfection as before. Now her vision was realized through complex, geometric designs. Conceptually interesting, her creatively amassed patterns, unleashed in a bold play of colours, fit together seamlessly and solemnly as if to provoke questions, opinions, or emotional reactions in the viewer. Unfortunately, not too many questions, opinions, or reactions were expressed to her. Again, she felt unfulfilled in her art and noticed that it had become somewhat derivative. Some other abstract painters appeared to follow her style, and she suspected that she might have unintentionally imitated others too.

Moreover, very few people showed any real interest in her elaborate paintings, much less acquired them, despite that it had been noticed—almost anointed—by a couple of local critics. But critical acclaim was not her passion. Nor even self-expression. She was interested in viewer response. Again, she left the palette behind and detached herself from her artistic pursuits. Just before leaving her city of Nara, she received a letter from Kyoto, Japan, with a short poem in it by Hiro. He was an independent, off-the-beaten-track poet and thinker, and her lifelong friend. On an old-fashioned piece of rice paper, using an outdated, calligraphy brush instead of an efficient computer keyboard, Hiro wrote in black ink:

A Brief History of Art

The long-lived friends—Harmony, Rhythm, Beauty, and Meaning,
Inevitably had become so culturally bored
With each classic other,
That they have temporarily resolved
To respectively, and mutually respectfully,
Impersonate Dissonance, Zigzag, Unsightliness, and Anti-sense
In order to become inclined
Towards creatively reinventing their fine, long-lived friendship,
At the hopefully higher tier of its original dimension
Until the velvety boredom returns,
With a degree of artistically expressed, slow paced vengeance.

Yoshi, who always liked and respected Hiro, was never much interested in his gently ironic poetry. Nevertheless, she found Hiro's dry text useful, when she considered her own path through the unchartered terrain of creative arts. She was wisely taking her time before shaping any pivotal decisions regarding what to paint and how to proceed.

Artists do not choose their art forms. It is the art that chooses the artist. There is not much choice. Predictably, Yoshi emerged from her retreat, born to paint. However, there was a distinct difference in her approach to art.

She had finally adopted the applied philosophy that *less is more.* Now, along with the image she painted, she pictured the person who would ultimately see the work. She had always felt that her pleasurable duty— privilege really—was to contribute to this viewer's internal life, even if for a very brief moment only. Yoshi's ideal had evolved from perfection to stimulating the best in her viewer. She wanted that stranger to think more, feel more, and enjoy more. Even one of those effects would be welcome as sufficient and rewarding to her.

She has carefully selected, from that time on, to paint small and unimposing elements from real life, but suspended in the Void, the rest to be filled with the viewer's imagination. The better to allow for creative thinking on the part of the viewer looking at her seemingly unfinished paintings, she thought. These paintings, or "brush elements of reality" as she would term them, seen as though returning from that indefinable void or readying to disappear into it again, were also meant to foster positive feelings.

Yoshi's natural, and never abandoned, search for harmonious perfection, coupled with her insight and professional experience, gave her work a genuine, if frugal, beauty. Her paintings were sophisticated expressions of modesty and simplicity. They instigated moments of quiet joy, however fleeting, in those who could spend time with them in silence.

Predictably, some of her peers among the photo-realism and abstract-expressionism schools, and a few of the critics, branded Yoshi a mere epigone of the old and outmoded school of Zen painting. She generally agreed with that opinion, but also thought her paintings differed from the ancient Zen works in various, reasonably detectable artistic regards. Indeed, they seemed to be at least original enough to be named by one critic as the "Zen-inspired Yoshi Nakamura painting style." Another insightful critic wrote of, "her ever potent, complex simplicity."

The media-dependent buyer-followers were not flocking to her miniature art gallery in a small Zen garden set on the bustling city's outskirts. However, discerning, self-directed clients did start visiting more frequently than before, even if just for a silent viewing. Some of them eventually decided to exchange their hard-earned money for these modest, but intriguing, paintings. Perhaps, Yoshi's art was starting to touch their own search for meaning in their lives.

Prudence

Prudence is born as the "brain-child"
From the mature union
Of responsibility, with diligence

Its usefulness is positively universal
Insofar as indispensable
For securing all a life really needs

The full-grown prudence falls in love
And courts spirituality—
Their "brain-child" is sheer success

Its apt existence models for others
Who through unfocused lives
In vain look for dreamt of fulfillment

In the history of literature there have been various authors writing either poetry or prose, who explored the theme of animals. Such writers use animals to portray relations among people. This literary technique allowed artists to convey a simplified, condensed message. Doing so, they would not ruffle sensitive social feathers. By the same token, they were shrewdly working around prickly criticism of the powers that be.

Among many others, French author La Fontaine, Polish author Krasicki, and the Russian, Krylow, masterfully pursued that genre. Much better known, British author Rudyard Kipling's *Jungle Books* were composed as fables to model human virtues like loyalty, friendship, and courage. The once very popular, twentieth-century British writer, George Orwell, analyzed the totalitarian political system (fortunately for him not immediately experienced) in *Animal Farm*, a satirical and exceptionally lucid vivisection.

Almost uniformly, the animals chosen by such authors for portraying human characters, belonged to nature's higher developed forms, from fish to heron, from raven to fox, from wolf to bear and lion, etc. It was Krylov, however, who reached for the remoter realm of insects to tackle the virtue of *prudence*. The beginning of his poem, "A Grasshopper and an Ant," translated here from the Russian, would more or less go as follows:

A playful grasshopper sang all summer long. It did not think about making provisions for the future, until the harsh winter's wind blew against its eyes. The fields turned clear and barren. The bright days, when under every leaf waited a table and a house, were gone ...

This sober poem juxtaposes the carefree attitude of the grasshopper against the prudent one of the ant. That ant worked hard all the summer, painstakingly securing its supplies in a safe place to quietly weather the winter. The late-asking-for-assistance, playful grasshopper was flatly refused by the ant, showed the door, and sent to meet the frost, ultimately perishing. Perhaps a less nineteenth-century-minded, less "Krilovian" or "Dickensian" and more compassionate, contemporary ant, if faced with a similar situation, would say something along these lines:

"I fully recognize that we are both insects. You really do not need to remind me that you are an innately delicate, colourful grasshopper, and I happen to be just a plain, resilient, uncomplicated ant. Yet, I believe in the solidarity of insects. The same solidarity you are eagerly fostering now, and also so eloquently appealing to. However, there is a fundamental difference between our respective assessments of your predicament—mine being that your misery comes courtesy of certain choices that you have made. Also, there is a significant difference in how we each understand the reasons for this unnecessary and uncomfortable conversation that should not be happening in the first place. You are making a convenient mental shortcut. You think that as I happen to have something important to you at the moment, and you do not, I should share it with you, just like that. However, your shortcut, though skilfully verbalized, does not exactly sound the way you want it to play, from my own perspective. How could it?

"In all due—but actually less than due—respect, you've got it quite wrong. I did not work this consistently and this hard just because I like to, as you prefer to think (so as to feel better about the wanting part of your character, I'd say). Trust me it was not my pleasurable quest for the heavenly sweet Turkish Delight wrapped in my hard work. So please forget projecting the essence of your own lightly-chosen pursuits on my arduous actions. And yes, I agree with you to a point. Some of my efforts were emotionally rewarding to me, but most of them simply required my sweat and blood. Frankly, I had to frequently drag myself to properly complete what I had started on time. In the meantime, you were where you were, doing what you were doing, or, just perhaps, not doing that much after all.

"In reality, you have lived as though to collect as many pleasurable, or exhilarating, moments as you could, and to avoid as many uncomfortable, grinding ones as you could manage. But the winter has come—as it predictably and inevitably does. In contrast, I chose to embark on a consecutive chain of consistent efforts, often ridden with unpleasant moments, rewarding myself with the pleasurable ones sparingly. All along keeping clearly in mind that the winter will arrive.

"Yes, I am an insect like you, so you are presumably as dear to me as I am to you. So ask yourself, but very honestly please, how dear am I to you, actually? Well, why to be suddenly so shy? True, I tend now to feel sorry for your unwisely self-induced situation, but extend those feelings to a very definite and obvious point where I stand. Until crossing that fine yet detectable line, you might have been just recklessly naive, possibly not having yet managed to learn basic prudence. By the same token, I will have no compassion for you as long as you continue to operate that way, crossing the said fine line. Behind it, semi-innocent naiveté ends, and the selfish roots of molasses-sweet entitlement eagerly establish themselves. Of course, only if allowed ...

"This winter, I will give you the benefit of the doubt. There is a policy in my household of two strikes, though; so be very careful how you conduct yourself. Now, I will let you in. If not, you would convert to an icicle very soon. However, taking refuge here over this harsh winter, you will cook for me, wash the dishes, clean my house daily, and clear the snow, as required. Ah, you will twice daily sing for me as well. After all, it would be an excellent opportunity for you to hone your relevant skills before summer comes. Then, I will let you go at early spring, so you can, hopefully, start realistically changing your pretty impractical ways.

"However, remember please what I say now: should you knock on my door again next winter, I will call the red warrior ants living nearby. They will be informed that you are disturbing the peace. Winter is a well-deserved time of peace for us tired, common black ants. During this important, calm period, many of us meditate about the sunny gate to the heaven of insects, so we should not be annoyed by anyone, even grasshoppers. I am sure that these restless and militant red ants would gladly take you in to their large barracks where they live and train. Once they do, I wish you the best of luck ...

"As for now, you have been advised. In the future, your safety, integrity, and well-being depend on how you choose to proceed. Well ... your intense silence tells me that, at least for now, you understand me perfectly. Nonetheless, try to memorize this awful feeling you are experiencing, standing by my door and getting increasingly angry—although not yet at yourself—having exposed yourself to my objective words. Remember very well this feeling and the entire scene you've volunteered for. It could help you get your act together. Come in, Grasshopper, you are welcome."

Part III

Garden of Shade

The fiend voices that rave, shall dwindle, shall blend,
shall change, shall become first a peace out of pain, then a light ...

—Robert Browning

The Trojan Horse

This lifelong campaign for survival, then growth,
Could require at times
Battling an adversary outside my body's thin walls

All such tangible "enemies" stay definitely easier
To identify and deal with,
Than the one camouflaged within the perimeter …

This inner enemy is more entrenched and subtle,
Hiding deep in my weakness
Which this shrewd foe converts into its own strength

Those outer foes may be forgiven, even befriended,
Unless they've made this inner one
To be their stealth and cunning "Trojan Horse"

If eclipsed from all sides, I will face a grave danger,
With my arch foe being the Horse
One to be burnt, before it blinds the truth within me

Seven Deadly Sins—*Sloth*

The turbid personality of sloth
Tends to evolve its two intricate specialties
That at times, are compelled
To act in temporary and sloppy collusion

The first specialty makes sure
That one does not do what has to be done
The remaining venue
Provides for the pursuit of what should end ...

When occasionally colluding,
Both opposite forces neutralize themselves,
Thus for a good while
Virtually nothing is really done, or not done

During such slump periods
Anxiety's bird pecks the windows often,
So sloth may integrate a bit
And get its trip-substances to avoid itself ...

A considerably aged and increasingly lonely owner of his own shadow has tended to spend long hours on a crooked bench in a rundown municipal park, opposite a century red-brick building of the Salvation Army. This daily vantage point has given him more privacy and better air than his lower bunk in a cramped basement dorm. The people passing by naturally assumed that the old and unkempt man talked to himself. They almost never sat beside him. When they did, it was for a short while only. He did *not* talk to himself, though. Unable—and then genuinely unwilling—to attract any company, he had found that talking to his *shadow* gave him a practical and convenient alternative. This particular cloudy morning, his faint shadow, wearing a worn-out baseball cap, started the following animated conversation:

"Oh my beloved master, did you ever have any good opportunities when you were young?"

"Cut the crap, pal; what are you up to today?" Blindsided, the owner of his shadow barked back defensively.

"Well, I have served you most faithfully all these long years, and it has been only recently that you have started relating to me," said the shadow. "I simply do not know much about your life. But for some strange reason I've found myself in a crowded shelter with many other depressed—and often rude—shadows ..."

"Oh my worthy, so loyally devoted servant," the unshaved owner began, feigning concern, "don't get me wrong. I will gladly answer all your clever questions, he said, pausing before launching in. "If you really want to know, my mom and dad were hard-working, but in fact pretty simple, poor people, so I did not feel like following their footsteps. Accordingly, I left home early, to go my own, smarter way. I think now that they may have loved me, or whatever. They tried and tried to contact me for years, but I responded only ... well, let's put it this way ... barely. Then they died. Being quieter than usual for a while, I caught the eye of a nice, honest girl with good values. I knew that she would die for me. Her name was Peggy—or maybe it was Patty—anyway something like that, and she had pretty, sweet eyes and a joyful, warm smile. But she wanted to have a family, and it is a hell of a lot of damned work to support one! So I left her, and she was, y'know, like devastated. Somehow I cannot forget the way she looked at me before I took off. See, I was quite a hunk back then, believe it or not ..."

"I believe, I believe," confirmed the shadow sardonically. "Even now, you look gorgeous."

"Shut up or I will stop talking to you! Besides, don't you ever forget who your master is," shouted the shadow's owner angrily, scaring a young woman passing by who thought he was addressing her.

"Oh my dear master, please accept my sincere apology," whinged the manipulative shadow. "Please try to forgive me, despite my so boorishly demonstrated shallow insensitivity ..." He paused, trying to think of another grovelling word to add, then changed tack. "And kindly continue your *uniquely fascinating* story."

"Okay, you smart ... whatever; where was *I*? Well, I had various jobs over the years, and did not feel like getting stuck with any. But once, I met a good boss who really believed in me and gave me a fair chance. He even promoted me on the job. See, at that time I was kind of stressed out, and started ... using. So, I lost that perfect opportunity soon enough. At least they sent me to rehab for free. There, this funny little lady-bug—in thick glasses—proved to me, after some boring psychological testing, that my IQ was quite high. Because of my 'potential' she talked me into finishing high school as an adult. I did that with flying colours. I even took some college courses—and excelled in them, believe it or not again!"

"Not only do I believe in you my master, but I also feel in my shadow of a heart that you are very wise," conveyed the shadow in such way that it was hard to figure out if he was serious or not. Nevertheless, the owner of his shadow decided to give him the benefit of the doubt. Due to that goodwill, the animated conversation on the battered wooden bench, surrounded by its occupant's exploited to the fullest cigarette butts, duly continued ...

"Well, I dropped those stupid courses. A few of them required much too much effort. Eventually ... off and on ... I had different jobs again, so, needless to say, had to move quite a lot. See, for some reason being stuck in one location or, worse, in one job always really got on my nerves somehow. Anyway, as I got older, those lousy jobs seemed to become harder and harder to get. Then I entered such a bleak period in my life that I did not want to talk even to you, my old shadow, about it," he said, downcast.

"After those bad, and then even worse, years, I ended up in that shelter. At first I volunteered a little in the nearby food bank, but it was always way too much work. See, those petty workaholics down there think that they just own you or something. Anyway, it was nice talking to you today, my hazy old buddy. Let's get up and move on now. Otherwise you will miss your prayer before my soup, and hey, today is beef-and-barley-broth day! But, you better hurry—this particularly cheap and unreasonably restrictive shelter does not have a hell of a lot of tolerance for your sloth!"

Seven Deadly Sins—*Gluttony*

Tied to its health-hostile extreme
The insatiable gluttony conditions itself
To fast expanding excess,
Being deftly oblivious to the agonies of hunger,
One struggling daily
At the life-threatening contrasting pole
Cursed with the tragic never-enough

For these two self-imprisoned
Whether the obese or the reed-thin one
Locked up in custody of their far extremes,
Freedom opens between these opposites only,
On the dignified path
Towards mastering an art of the just-sufficient

It is an enormous challenge for frail hunger
To climb the peak of the just-sufficient
The so-far-lucky gluttony
May, for a change, reflect on the pains
Experienced by hunger
Then regain health with integrity
Deciding to stay slightly hungry after each meal
Perhaps—even—*donate food.*

Personable, competitively shrewd Cornelius has danced his way up the CEO
ladder with grace. His industry had just started forming its particular bubble,
so the investors' "lemming-money" continued to pour in. As he climbed, his
derivative electronic assets did too. Even better, the entire monetary system
was slowly blowing the mother of all bubbles. Both times and things were
great. Under the circumstances, it was no wonder that Cornelius took genuine
interest in luxurious glitz, conducting extensive "field research" into it. He
went through power-everything—the oversized mansions, sleek cars, and
pleasure yachts.

   Somehow not quite fulfilled, however, his ambition turned to looking
for his own signature niche; he discovered that his true penchant had to do
with his taste buds. He had become an aficionado of top quality food. Utterly
uncompromising, Cornelius researched the most expensive foods offered

by über-posh restaurants. After extensive dedicated sampling, he short-listed the critically anointed restaurants and dishes that most appealed to his increasingly refined palate, including a long list of mogul-friendly wines. Being health-smart, he then prudently consulted the locally celebrated trinity of a traditional medical doctor, an organic, homeopathy one, and the dietician guru of all dietician gurus. Together, they pointed him to the healthiest fare. His passion was heartfelt and artful indeed.

Healthy, lean, and energetic, he unknowingly managed to beat a world's record: namely, his daily restaurant bill. It could easily have bought a day's worth of food for an entire third-world village, except that it did not. Today, before entering the monumental doors of a famous slow-food "temple," he briefly looked with more disgust than pity at a sloppily dressed *fatso*, apparently making his way to the fast-food establishment around the corner. Cornelius put him out of his mind, so as not to put him off his meal. His preoccupied mind, after deciding to order the *salade de pissenlits avec croutons* for an appetizer, and *pissaladiere* for dessert, was skilfully scanning the anticipated, highly inspired main course options.

As for the slob heading for the fast-food joint, Bob did not think much of the smartly bodied and dressed snob swallowed by the double doors of the fancy-fared Platinum Pit. He had plenty on his preoccupied mind too. Having already had a generous helping of eggs and bacon, with a handsome tower of snow-white toast for breakfast, he was hungry again. Fortunately, lunch was not too far off. Today, Bob felt like going for the triple-decker, but not being born yesterday, he knew very well that they didn't make such things. Walking slowly with some strain and heavy breathing, he resolved that it would be neat to beat the system and get two double-deckers instead. These would be accompanied by two super-sized portions of french fries and a jumbo Coke, or preferably two, given the sticky-hot and smoggy, grey day.

However, things were a bit more complicated. A decision—ridden with certain consequences—had to be arrived at: whether to return here for dinner or get take-out now. If he opted for the take-out solution, Bob could get *three* double-deckers and top them off with a sundae, in turn topped off with an irresistibly sweet layer of dense, brown caramel, and eat back at the rooming house. Just before entering the bright, cheerfully appointed fast-food-cookie-cutter neighbourhood "chapel," and still deep in thought, he began leaning towards this more reasonable take-out option. It would free him from the undesirable chore of walking here twice, even though carrying the necessary amount of regular Coke home would be quite punishing too. Accordingly, the desired outcome would not be, unfortunately, an entirely win-win situation … *But on the other hand,* he thought, deep in his quandary, *who ever said that life doesn't suck? Man, it sure does. Oh yeah, it does—like why on earth, did they not only suspend my driving licence after maybe a couple of beers or so, but also seize my roomy clunker right there on the spot?* Which "they" did, though it was so perforated by rust, that it looked more like a bulky piece of metal artwork than a car.

Finally, separated by the thick glass of their different social and financial stations, the two perfect strangers, Cornelius and Bob, became equal brothers-in-arms—or respectively, in silver versus plastic forks. At the very same time, they were both losing to the exact same adversary: gluttony, whether expressed through so-called quality or quantity. Their potential inner ally weakening with each bite, though, was their self-reflection, whether on the battlefields of seductively subjective quality, or so succulently objective, irresistible quantity …

Seven Deadly Sins—*Greed*

The addicted to expansion tree of greed
Evolves much too thin and shallow roots only,
Since it grows on the poorest soil
Of non-fertile insecurity

Its trunk surely looks impressive,
But is hollow and full of hardworking insects
Eagerly chewing up their habitat.

The fast-developing too long branches
Extend as far as it gets,
Dangerously overstretched in to-be-owned … air
Straining the weak root system

Sooner—rather than later
This covertly ailing tree suddenly falls,
Due to the masterly built-in structural imbalance …

"Being a man of honour, I've never given any interviews to you liars and once, in my 'heroic' past, even got a couple of paparazzi shot at … But today I've changed my mind, thinking fondly about the always so firmly loyal to the Family and its business model, never wavering goodness of my full-figured late mamma. You will not publish it anyway, therefore who cares? Otherwise, I like your intelligent and, yes, properly respectful first question, 'What made you a man of success?'"

Well, in hot pursuit of my self-actualization, I drove up and down the fast lane on the—let's put it bluntly—winding highway of my wild and free life. It dawned on me, though, while singing solo for the deputy warden or in the prison chapel's large, pumpkin-colour choir, that I must stop making money through crime. I mean, of course, *dis*organized crime. See, I've been hooked on money for quite a while now—I sort of hate to admit it, but not unlike the pervert who ruminates about his dirty things, I fantasize about dough. It's all clean, however, just an innocent picture of fresh, crisp dough. Those cute, newly printed, and tightly banded bundles are the most attractive to me for some reason. Well, that is just who I am, or the way things are and sure will remain to be, at least as far as I am concerned.

That is precisely why I prudently decided to invest in my education.

I entered some demanding and cumbersome studies, completed all the required courses, seminars, and field placements, and then passed the final exams *cum laude*. Yes, I thwarted my death from them all—the outwitted late boss, the faithful competition, the chasing my car police shooting in self-defence, and even the high-maintenance clients that lashed out with razors. I've arrived, securing a very-hard-to-get diploma of a drug-squad-registered, big-time drug dealer.

Now, I own a huge stable of the disorganized punks that I used to despise. I operate as a public servant of sorts, just off the government's grid. Therefore I can afford to not be too anal about the conflict-of-interest thing. So, I allow these low-life punks to double-dip, since many of my employees serve as my clients as well. I have to keep them reined in a bit, though, so they don't slide down too fast.

I once watched that pathetic musical-dud, *The Lion King*, and simply giggled—I've accomplished much better than that. I've wild-caught, tamed, and groomed a sizeable squad of those hyena characters, and put them to good use. In my line of duty, I have to keep a close eye on them, though. Under my careful watch, they properly train and support the sales staff to supply the market at high professional standards. This squad can play and replay that funny "Wilhelm Tell" piece for me, shooting the bad apples, with their hyena-eerie laughter, which I, for some reason, viscerally enjoy. You know, no one appreciates the price I've paid. Nobody cares about my sacrifices, and the efforts I had to exert while establishing my healthily growing, shrewdly organized business, which many have been trying to destroy. In spite of their blatant ill will, I thrive as a reliable, grudgingly respected, well-connected entrepreneur. You would be surprised to learn how high up the ladder I am, but I will tell you this much—the cops do not possess the God-given monopoly to "have things" on some high-up, fancy folks ... I, in contrast, use such sensitive information for blackmailing.

Like any other prudent, busy executive I care about my company, as they say, 24-7. It is only the occasional night that I wake up in a cold sweat, having that recurrent dream. In this nightmare, I walk down a long bridge in the dark, but then stop, paralysed with an awful, mortal fear. Then a skeleton-thin, young drug addict in rags—with my death in his angry eyes—grabs me by my gold chain to slit my throat. During such bad nights, I tend to cope in my own—I have to admit—rather peculiar way. Namely, I put on a newer gold chain, from my vast collection. I do that in front of my full-length mirror, splendid in its gold-plated rococo frame. This ritual behaviour somehow makes me to feel wonderful about myself, except for noticing that perhaps my hips might have grown slightly full-figured.

Afterwards I may watch the best from my extensive and believe me, very well-diversified skin library. Then I have a drink or ten, or go for a walk to get some fresh air and trim the body, one supposedly morbidly obese according to my little quack. Other than that, your interview is over. I feel like going to my custom Caesar-sized bed now. By the way, if you would ever try to describe my business, or attempt to trace the quality products regularly delivered on public demand and in good faith, to any so called "criminal activities," I will laugh right in your naively self-righteous face.

Once, someone like you was alleging in a certain puny article that my deliveries were allegedly linked to 666 (or so) homicides, suicides, invalids, orphans, terminal infections, fires, incarcerations, divorces, and so on … That crazy journalist was even extending his yap-yap about my further "ripple effect." Oh, he did not like his too delicate feet in the bucket with fast hardening concrete before plunging, I can tell you this much … What's more, surprise, surprise, he did not get, poor thing, any post-mortem Pulitzer Prize either. See where I am coming from? So, just in case, I will make sure, before retreating to my palatial bedroom through my stately mirror-gallery, to pass your home address to my giggly hyena-boys. No offence pal, but business is business, and money is money, you know. Before I talk to them, I may first take a walk on the nearby bridge, although it is quite similar to the one I've seen in my nightmares, and it is already pitch dark outside …

Seven Deadly Sins—*Lust*

Lust breeds like locusts,
Acts at the mercy of its own impulses,
Hence, if not reigned in,
Quickly overpowers moral judgment,
Removes basic realism,
Takes away security,
With personal integrity
Blowing with the wind of social scrutiny
All the slippery way along

Within the art of one's life
The skilfully tamed lust, harnessed well,
Adds the rainbow of the sensual
To the insipid black-and-white palette
But if wild, may convert
A person into a condemned "bull"
Stimulated by the crimson cloth
Of that sleek toreador
Or—the lust-hungry demon

In that old isolated prison, where I worked as a psychologist, the unit for sex offenders was particularly lively. Its reluctant dwellers, often highly emotionally charged individuals, represented diversified nationalities, races, and ethnic backgrounds. Short but muscular, Bruce happened to be the rarest indeed case of an Aboriginal there. Unlike the others, they were extremely rarely represented in that unit. The penetrating gaze of his small eyes, along with his decisive facial features, sent a clear message that he was a concrete thinker. He was also, certainly, a doer. Sure enough, Bruce soon transformed the entire dark corridor into a fiefdom of his own. In order to keep the vassals in due check, he heralded allegedly having a black belt in the martial arts. Poignantly making his point, he used to powerfully kick the walls during his "training sessions," so others would notice his skills. With power, favours came. He helped himself to other men's canteen, and enforced sexual favours against the younger inmates.

A reliable little jailbird had already sung into my ear that Bruce was lately lusting for an angelic-looking kid named Shawn, who, scared stiff, was being forced to serve as a sex slave. Little birds are known for beautifully singing, but not for formally testifying. Still, I consulted with the institution's security. Because no one was coming forward, fearful of Bruce, all the authorities could do was to hold him in Segregation for a couple of days. Their hands were legally tied; they could not act on some vague allegation. It looked like I could also do no more, so I just gave up. However, the picture of that terrified kid bothered me. As a result, I decided to use what I call "trench psychology," in hopes off nabbing Bruce. His latest victim's sentence was to expire within some two months.

I went to the Segregation Unit to talk to Bruce one-on-one. He showed up all tense, not knowing what was going on, as nobody had charged him with anything. Needless to say, his desire to reclaim his fiefdom was virtually burning in him. Our distinctly uncomplicated and fact-oriented short therapeutic session went exactly as follows:

Client: What the … is going on?! I'm not staying in this … hole!

Therapist: It was me who sent you here. No freebie canteen anymore. And, just maybe, no sex for now. On the other hand, Bruce, didn't you have too much sex lately anyway?

Client: You … goof! I'll make sure to get you when I get out!!
At this time, pale Bruce boiled with hatred, and approached me in a directly threatening manner.

Therapist: You are welcome. Is it the truth that you kept sexually assaulting other guys on the unit?
Feeling insulted, Bruce did not answer, but started posturing a shadow-fight in front of my desk. I seemed to be on a good track and needed to strike while the iron was hot.

Therapist: They say that you got that "pink belt" or something. Did you really get it? Bruce leaned on my desk. He was not talking intelligibly anymore; just swearing, and started intermittently throwing fast forceful air-punches with his right and left hands. He would stop about one inch from both sides of my head. I realized how he enforced compliance on his range. His eyes radiated sparks of fury emanating from his suffering soul. The corners of his swearing mouth were starting to show a little bit of foam.

Therapist: Well, Bruce, you go ahead and see what happens …
His eyes very briefly focussed on mine, and he sorted out that I was not afraid of him. Fearful enough of other things, I had difficulty being afraid

of people, which incidentally was handy in my line of work. Maybe it was because, in a way, I loved all of them regardless, while detesting their attitudes and behaviour. Then Bruce glanced at my hands on the desk, and clearly did not like what he saw. They were, still, the rough hands of a former labourer. Perhaps, an equally indelicate mentality could follow?

Not knowing what to do, Bruce resolved to make an expression of spitting at my face, but ultimately did not dare do it. Finally, to save face, infuriated and pale, he abundantly spit on my notepad instead, and stormed out of the interview room. *There, I got him!* I asked the guards who were standing by to formally witness that he spat in my direction, and I wrote the relevant occurrence report.

He would stay in solitary for investigation and serve an institutional charge afterwards. I did not lay any "street charge" against Bruce. In the meantime the "sweet kid," Shawn, would get out, hopefully learning his lesson that one must not extort from sugar daddies living in their big houses. If offending again, Shawn could get in an even bigger house an equally lustful but much rougher daddy, one that may not exactly sugar-coat ...

A month later, Bruce put in a request to see me. We met in the same room. At this time he did not posture or shadow-fight; he just sat on the chair on the other side of my desk. He seemed calm and, unlike before, looked at me with no hate, but maybe even with a degree of respect, since I had stood up to him. Then he said, "I've made something for you," and gave me a chessboard drawn on thick cardboard and a full set of chess pieces. The crayon-coloured figures were painstakingly crafted from a compound made of chewed-up bread mixed with toilet paper, all glued with his saliva and then dried. Much surprised, I thanked him. He did not feel like talking, and returned to his cell. After all, Bruce had always been a doer, not a talker.

After some eight weeks in segregation he returned to his cellblock. According to my reliable little bird's cheerful song, he behaved more or less acceptably. He put in a request to see me again. Then we enjoyed a number of short and refreshingly uncomplicated therapy sessions, like the one below:

Therapist: Why did you do all those unsuccessful robberies, Bruce?

Client: What the ... you mean?

Therapist: No offence; I am just curious. It is your life anyway, and you are a big boy.

Client: I needed money.

Therapist: We all need it. Wearing your shoes, Bruce, I would rather work for my money.

Client: It's very hard to get a job where I live, you don't understand a thing.

Therapist: I simply feel sorry to see a young, healthy, and strong man be a beggar.

Client: Are you crazy or what?! I'm not a beggar!! Maybe you are a … … beggar?

Therapist: Robbing is just a violent form of begging. You try to get something from others that you did not work for. The only difference being that you have a weapon in your begging hand, so now you beg violently.

Client: [Nothing was said, just angry silence.]

Therapist: Let's forget about robbing for now. You had also committed some sexual assaults in the past too. Why?

Client: What you mean why? I got drunk and maybe some things happened.

Therapist: Booze never triggers anything in us we did not harbour a potential for inside. Most people who get drunk do not do anything like that. They do not assault others sexually. If you agree with this simple logic, do you intend to work on getting rid of that potential once and for all?

Client: [Angry silence, with nothing said.]

Therapist: Sorry to say, Bruce, from my perspective, you were violently begging not only for money, but even for sex. Raping, is just sexually begging in the most unsightly of all imaginable ways. Someone clearly rejects your body, but you keep enforcing it on that person, surely making it therefore, say, as repulsive as puke to any individual you attack with your violent begging for sex. Again, really sorry to say it, but you used to be in fact a double beggar. All your ancestors were tough warriors and hunters. How do you know that they do not watch you, when you do your stuff? If they do, would they be proud or highly offended and deeply disgusted? I understand that your dad hunts deer and moose for a living …

Client: Enough of your ... crap! I've got to go!

But he kept coming back ... When he was to be discharged in one week, our last no-nonsense, reality-therapy session came. He brought a second gift. This time it was a small eagle with stretched-out wings, carved in white soap. His carving was objectively artful! Surprised again, I sincerely thanked him. By the end of that wrap-up session, we cracked a few, properly unrefined jokes. Then I bid him farewell, "Bruce, you watch out, man. If you ever return here, I will personally beat you up!"

He looked at me for a couple of seconds, unsure whether it was a joke or not. Then we just laughed, having the same comical picture in our minds, of a clichéd dangerous offender being pounded on by his clichéd meek shrink. At that stage of our distinctly uncomplicated therapeutic relationship, he knew well that I genuinely not only respected but also liked Aboriginals, while reserving my right to deeply disrespect and dislike sexual violence demonstrated by any person. We shook hands goodbye. Just before he left the office, I told him, "Take my best advice, Bruce, and talk very honestly about everything to your Elder up north. He will keep your secrets. I will be far from you, I am not good enough in comparison, anyway. He knows your ways and needs much better than I do. Will you do it?"

"Okay," he agreed, "I will talk to one guy."

Bruce, who used to be our annual if not perennial flower in the behind-bars variety garden, was never seen here again. Some years later, that old and isolated prison with the bustling block for sex offenders got decommissioned. I still have Bruce's chess kit. It obviously required a lot of work and goodwill to make. The artful, small soap-eagle gradually melted down over the successive hot summers, starting with the sharp contours of its wings, and then to the predatory beak and claws. Presumably, Bruce mellowed down too. He may well have gotten a job and a family by now, instead of being buried in some forgotten prison. Hopefully, he at last defeated his inner enemy of the uncontrolled lust that enslaved him, and forced him to power-trip through sexually acting out.

Maybe his corridor-famous belt in martial arts, whether black or indeed pink, had helped him to win that most difficult fight of his life—who knows? All I know is that I hope that Bruce walked away from our—let's be honest—not overly sophisticated therapeutic encounters, lusting for a better life.

Seven Deadly Sins—*Wrath*

On average, self-doubt—if frustrated with others
In a natural way attempts to protect itself
Through utilizing innate safety valves
For its own anger's energy, bubbling deep inside

But the helpless long-brewing and toxic self-hate
When set to discharge its compressed force
Pushes the red-hot button, instantly resulting
In a volcanic eruption of pure wrath blown out

Its conscience-less lava blindly commits arson
To the short-lived triumph mortally engulfing
The still breathing, moving, vulnerable house
For a lone shivering soul, with no roof, no walls

The raging flames of the fast spent wrath's force
Die down, soon extinguished by sharp, icy fear
Then it takes all the time until one's own death
To try and try forgetting, somewhere, somehow,
About that black raven, in silence hovering
Above one's numb memory—quasi-frozen land ...

Yesterday, I saw this young, tall, and handsome man on the TV news. His "making-sure-to-get-caught" escape from the crime scene, ended in the camera-friendly climactic chase by several police cars on a busy highway. Now we sit alone in a small and bare room, its walls painted white. This room is just one of many other like it, well protected from daylight's intrusion into the large and stern building. Three days ago, he drove to the victims' house. While there, he stabbed his small children to death in front of their mother, his ex-wife, punishing her for having rejected him. Then he killed her as well. I am his prison psychologist. He is my first case of the day, put on suicide-watch by a nurse because the rare severity of his crime. She had logically assumed that he might become suicidal once he realizes what he has done.

He presents as somewhat withdrawn, cooperative, polite, and remarkably collected. His almost expressionless eyes look at me, but they do not really see. I look at him, and the strange thought, *Who dwells in you?* crosses my mind. We talk a bit and I learn, among other things, that he "got very angry and, kind of, lost it." Overall, the situation is by and large straightforward. If I remove him from suicidal watch, he may kill himself—or not. My job is to make no mistake here. It would be ultimately costly to him … It would also be costly, both emotionally and administratively, to all stakeholders beginning with me. If not putting him off watch, I would need to see this handsome man tomorrow, and deal with the above situation again. I decide not to remove the precautions for now, and assess some other inmate who after receiving a typical "Dear John" letter ended up on suicidal watch.

The next day, the still cooperative and polite man who killed his immediate family sits in front of me in the same small, bare room again, dressed in his off-white protective tunic—in prison slang, "baby dolls." He looks a little bit tired, yet comes across as reasonable and calm and making progress in adjusting to his new circumstances. We talk more, mostly about life. I put him through all the overt and covert investigations, carefully matching the content of his answers with the tone of his voice and his body language, including facial expressions. He passes.

Now I apply the final "danger-filter" that I have invented after some years on the job at this prison. First, I concentrate to my available best, becoming all ears and eyes, amplified. Then I ask the short question, "Do you think that you need this suicide-watch?"

His "No" is not delayed and is unqualified. It does not suggest any overtone of concealed hesitancy; feeling genuinely spontaneous. Crucially, his eyes do not avoid, even for a second or two, my eyes, fixed on his. Given his presentation, I resolve to sign him off suicide-watch. Now I give him some routine information like, "You can take a shower, wear regular clothing, and get a mattress. Then you can call your family."

He looks at me with an expression, one difficult to describe, which under different circumstances might have been construed as a slight, sad smile, and calmly says, "I just killed my family."

Damn it! I have made a mistake. Now he may think about them tonight, feel unbearably guilty, and then try to slash or hang himself. I take a breath and my experience prevails over my concern: He will think about them, regardless. Persons with his type of personality do not tend to hurt themselves, although they may hurt or, at times, even kill others.

Indeed, no mistake has been made. From his point of view, we are simply exchanging germane information, polite enough, and ultimately inconsequential. In this particular case, I do not make any plans for additional psychological follow-up, other than the routine session. He appears to have accepted his fate of spending life in prison, likely being a quite trouble-free inmate if left undisturbed by others. Hopefully, his capacity for wrath, now dormant in him and not easy to understand, will never again be demonstrated to its blind extreme.

This very young, short, and slim man, wearing his "baby-doll" tunic while sitting in the familiar, small, bare room, killed his brother yesterday with a pair of scissors. Because there were no multiple victims, and no spectacular car chase on the highway, he just made a short note in a newspaper. During the admission process, he confessed to a very strong urge to take his own life. Accordingly, he was escorted directly to the Segregation Unit and put on suicide-watch. He is still unable to collect himself. Doubled over in utmost desperation, he sobs uncontrollably, his face hidden in his two trembling palms. He is markedly shaking and totally unable to talk; he will need to be seen again tomorrow.

The next day inevitably comes. He sits in front of his correctional psychologist in a small room that has seen and heard it all. He didn't sleep, thinking all night about his dead brother, and still feeling that there is no reason to continue with his own life. During the awful, long night he cried so much that the tears do not readily come anymore; his sobbing is all inside. I provide him with a brief and routine crisis-intervention, and don't terminate his suicide-watch.

Predictably, we briefly talk again the next day. The inmate explains that he did not mean it. His brother started picking on him, which he used to do for many years, back to childhood. This time, though, he did it in the presence of his friends. He felt humiliated and became very angry. Still, he did not start the fight. He just "said things." That's when the physical fighting quickly took over. His brother unintentionally got hurt during the course of it … somehow, but he left the scene afterwards, seemingly all right. It was only after he covered some distance that, all of a sudden, he fell … and died. The story brings a new burst of tears, making further conversation impossible. The bereft inmate is escorted to his cell, and stays on watch.

On the forth day, he presents exhausted, but somewhat calmer. I manage to direct our halting conversation along the normal route. As I'd hoped, he starts talking about his parents. I do my best to prove to him that presently he is all they have, so his life is the most precious treasure they are left with.

He listens, but asks, "How could they love me at all after what I have done?"

Since I am convinced that they could, I tell him, what I think, hoping to get through on some level. He says nothing, but his body language and the expression on his pained face seem to drop some small margin of the terrible burden he is carrying. It looks like he might need only one more day on suicide-watch.

The fifth day of his ordeal on a cold concrete bunk comes. We talk longer today, and I put him subtly through the entire drill. He comes out cleared. His suicide-watch can be safely terminated, with my referral to multi-discipline professional follow-up. I make a plan to see him for several psychological follow-up sessions as well. He might benefit from counselling that explains how he is not the Cain he feels himself to be, but an Abel who survived. If he wants to develop himself now, he must start working very seriously on anger management. I know his open emotional wound will heal one day. But the deep scar will remain in him for the rest of his life. If he uses it wisely, the passing time remains his most effective ally.

Seven Deadly Sins—*Envy*

A man that hath no virtue in himself, ever envieth virtue in others.
                                                              —Francis Bacon

The concealed flower of budding envy
Gives the truthful testimony to one's own inability
To ever accomplish
What someone else just naturally enjoys

It slowly grows as its object, with an innate ease,
Attains the desirable goals,
Floridly blossoms
When others notice, and applaud that success

Then, the venom-green flower of envy
Either detaches from pain's target for good,
Or exhales bitter-toxins
Eliminating the witness, to one's own life failures …

Anton and Wolfgang developed their lifelong friendship while studying chemistry at the same institute, in the historic city of Vienna. If contrast in personalities can make friends more attractive and complementary to each other, these two were a living testimony to the possibility.

Energetic Anton had always been perfectly organized, focused, and consistent in everything he chose to pursue. His naturally executed self-control, stemming from remarkable willpower and personal ambition, allowed him to become a highly accomplished student. Although not a brilliantly imaginative or spectacularly creative person, he was quick in acquiring a broad body of knowledge in the chemistry field. Moreover, he displayed a specific ability that was invaluable to his career. Namely, he always knew how to say the right thing to the right person in the right place and, crucially, at the right time. Not surprisingly, he was elected president to the local association of students by a landslide majority, and then tapped to pledge in an exclusive stepping-stone fraternity.

Meticulous Anton managed to invite himself to the exclusive inner circle of famous professor Maria Theresa K. An internationally acclaimed chemist-humanist, K enjoyed a nearly divine status among both the chemistry students and the youngest, still unjaded faculty members. Working for K in the mystifying Laboratory of Humanistic Neo-Chemistry in the nineteenth-century attic on the fourth floor was a sweet dream come true. Even taking the oath of allegiance to her and to humanism, required from each new employee and posted under the portrait of Maria Sklodowska-Curie in K's cluttered office, added to the ennobling feeling of uniqueness and scientific exclusivity indeed.

Rounding out his promising picture, Anton easily became captain of the student-popular soccer team. As such, he was featured at least once in the sports section of a certain Viennese newspaper, not to mention frequent exposure in the student newsletter. Anton was impressive—the consummate, blond-haired, long-legged, bright, and athletic young man. Built like an acrobat, skilled in social repartee, whether you liked him or not, you had to admit he was a distinctly intelligent and handsome gentleman. That's why it was so unexpected when his girlfriend, Ingrid, left him. Neither her family, nor her friends, who all respected Anton, could fathom her irrational explanation. She said she had "become uncomfortable with something disquieting in his eyes." Everyone agreed she was simply over-sensitive.

Shaken, Anton felt compelled to take under his wide, strong wing the seemingly lame-duck Wolfgang. He genuinely wanted to protect him from the collegial teasing and practical jokes that some other students routinely bestowed upon Wolfgang. On the other hand, could he? It's sad, but there are those individuals who, regardless of what they do or don't do, seem to entice insensitive others to tease or ostracize them. Wolfgang obviously belonged to that group. It undoubtedly started with his looks. He was short and plump, except for his skinny and restless extremities. They were all too often finding their way to disrupt the order of things around him, be it a mug with hot coffee on the table, or a sugar bowl he was attempting to politely pass to someone. Was it any wonder that his sweater was permanently marked by stains, and his shirt often dotted with traces of involuntary droppings from his too talkative mouth?

The irregular facial features he was endowed with by Mother Nature, and she happened to be thrifty in his particular case, were not helpful either. His dark eyes could have been described as warm, or pleasantly dreamy, if it they had not been so bulgy and annoyingly unfocused, flitting constantly away from whoever he was talking to. In the same vein, Wolfgang's unkempt hairdo may have been seen by others as somehow bohemian or perhaps "artistic." Unfortunately, the specks of dandruff piling in drifts on his shoulders did not foster it. Plus, his sallow face, with puffy cheeks and a double chin, harmonized too well with all the unappealing rest. To be fair to Wolfgang, he was harmless and cheerful in his own, lost to the material world, way. Unfortunately, even that backfired on him. His friendly smiles and polite, often witty, remarks readily revealed his teeth, which did not match his young age particularly well.

Despite it all or maybe because of it, Anton developed genuinely friendly feelings towards his awkward, gullible, and presumably ineffective colleague. He even attempted to help him out of his timid, odd shell. For example, he often modelled for Wolfgang how to chat with others and relax, drinking white wine in small restaurants clustered along the winding, lively streets; how to engage in funny, casual banter with attractive girls they might meet while strolling down the promenade along the Danube River. All in all, they increasingly enjoyed their time together, exchanging their dreams about the future, their careers plans, or pending projects and assignments. However, that good, friendly feeling did not apply to one particular place in which they had to spend long hours together.

In his sadly circumvented social life, Wolfgang was disorganized, forgetful, chronically late, and reliably chaotic. In addition, his money-management skills, unlike Anton's, were dismal. All such limitations appeared to miraculously vanish in the chemistry lab. Working in science, Anton's clumsy friend turned into a wizard. This was a mysterious stranger, an impressive Wolfgang that totally puzzled Anton. It was here only that Wolfgang's uncoordinated hands became precise and his movements purposeful in conducting consecutive sequences. Most important, his finely executed decisions inevitably resulted in the best possible outcomes. If Anton was very good at it, his friend rose above that. He was *excellent*.

There must have been something more to it, as Anton intelligently inferred, thinking one night about Wolfgang. Anton definitely liked working in the lab, no problem there. Wolfgang, on the other hand, was passionate about it; loving the whole process, and would become totally consumed by it. Had that been the reason why Professor Kaiser, the science goddess, who rarely visited their basement lab, stopped short in front of the naively oblivious Wolfgang, lingering to observe his busy hands? Since that event, Anton began thinking about his talented, if awkward, friend more often and watching his work more attentively than before.

Chemical experimentation not withstanding, the two well-cultivated youths shared yet another passion in common: classical music, including opera. Visiting the famous Viennese State Opera House to hear and watch Giuseppe Verdi's *Othello* was by no means an inexpensive venture, especially for students. Obviously, Anton had to lend money to Wolfgang, who was broke as usual, always giving his money away, expecting no repayment, and likewise not paying his own debts. Anton almost regretted paying his way again until they unexpectedly met two interesting girls at the opera house who enjoyed classical music as well. These two would change their lives.

Ilza and Helga were close girlfriends, both studying art history. Ilza, to whom Anton felt attracted the moment they met, was already working part-time in the *Kunsthistorishes* museum. She was tall, good looking, and soon challenged the smitten Anton to skiing with her in the high Alps. She was better at it than he, but he took consolation in his unquestionable accomplishments playing soccer. She soon grew attracted to sensible and handsome Anton and before long, they began dating quite regularly. If anyone could fall in love in a rational, sober, and fully realistic way, Anton and Ilza did just that, exemplifying an exception to the typical rule of irrational love. What was important to them was that they clearly felt like they fit together in terms of values, economic and social ambitions, professional plans, and eventually planning a family, which they seriously talked about well in advance.

In contrast, shy Helga appeared to be something of a "female Wolfgang." Not as good looking or self-confident as energetic Ilza, Helga nonetheless had a timidly warm smile, a pleasant timbre to her voice, gentle manners, and large green eyes that unmistakeably revealed a unique inner light lit within her. Anton noticed it, but it hit Wolfgang with such a force of love—or destiny—that he found the courage to lovingly reach out for her. Clearly, thought Anton, something was in his clumsy little friend, perhaps dormant and undetectable heretofore, but it seemed to command a reciprocal, equally loving embrace from Helga.

Wolfgang and Helga quickly became an almost inseparable couple, enjoying as much time together as possible. In contrast, Anton and Ilza had started spending less time in common. They amicably decided that, while making plans for the future together, they would prefer not to hamper each other's private lives, by now well correlated, but still somewhat distant nevertheless.

Under the circumstances, Anton and Wolfgang naturally disengaged a bit. Seeing each other less often did not diminish their mutual, warm friendship though. They still met to chat about their lives, newly unfolding events, and their soon-to-be-realized professional careers. Their studies were about to conclude, after passing their daunting final exams. It was during one of these occasions that Anton suddenly experienced a different emotion towards his good friend Wolfgang …

They were sitting in a tiny garden restaurant, sipping Riesling wine. Anton noticed that Helga very naturally and gracefully touched Wolfgang's face ever so softly. And it pained him. It was as though her large eyes sent a gentle wave of profound, unconditional love towards his bulging, as usual too unfocused eyes. Did she not see how objectively repulsive they were? Why had his Ilza—at the moment attentively looking into a miniature mirror to correct her impeccable makeup—never touched him in such a way? What on earth did this delicate and, let's admit, pretty Helga see in her "laughingstock" Wolfgang? True, he was a very good chemist, but what about the substandard, pathetic *rest* of him?

Anton pushed away this sudden and uncomfortable emotion, ashamed for even having such brief thoughts. He, smoothly as ever, reengaged in their friendly conversation. However, some subtle residue of his jealousy was not easily swept under the carpet and found its deposit deep in his mind. Over the next couple of nights he had a recurring and painful dream about it.

He could not fathom what Helga saw in such an unattractive and ineffective man. She must truly love him for something specific, but what was it? Anton would still prefer to be with his socially astute, conventionally attractive Ilza, than with that impractical, moonstruck—if interesting—Helga. It was only that he … and he was only reluctantly admitting this to himself … wished that Ilza could express her feelings towards him the same way Helga did to Wolfgang. Yes, he also would not mind it at all, if others would see such a spontaneous, enviable expression of genuine love. His social instincts were telling him, though, that it was Wolfgang who got lucky, not him. Anton's friendship towards Wolfgang did not noticeably change, but he started to perceive it via new lenses. Somehow it was becoming less rewarding.

Then the day came that Anton would never forget. They were completing a complex experiment, the lab part of their final exams. All students were assigned to a team and supervised by their colleagues' team leaders—those who had achieved the best marks in the two final semesters. Predictably, Anton and Wolfgang assumed such roles, each leading one of the separate competing teams.

The challenging task was to figure out the right proportions among various chemical ingredients in a compound. They had to be properly matched. Then the optimal time sequences were to be designed for mixing them, applying at every stage the varying degrees of heat. Each step perfectly performed to trigger the planned chemical reaction. The time of the successful completion of that reaction, as well as the quality of the evolved final product, were to be assessed by a computer. Its monitor was placed on a somewhat baffling, small, but distinct structure, known to some insiders as the field altar to humanistic neo-chemical sciences.

For all the team leaders, the stakes were high, as professor Maria Theresa K herself was to descend from the attic to their basement and attend the grand finale. She already announced through Herr Pritzl, the plain but highly influential old janitor and her very close personal confidant, that she would select her two new assistants from the three lucky winners.

Self-assured Anton was working evenly, in his characteristically systematic manner, properly utilizing all his acquired knowledge, leaving nothing to chance. Everything appeared to be progressing seamlessly. He watched with some hidden satisfaction as Wolfgang seemed to be experimenting within the experiment, losing precious time to alter his working strategy several times. Suddenly, all of it started to marvellously pay off. With a growing feeling of misfortune, Anton realized that entranced Wolfgang was ahead of him. To add insult to injury, that unlikeable career-absorbed, cold, and dry fish, Greta, who dwelled like a domesticated mouse in the library, was also advancing at a threatening pace.

As expected, the janitor—ennobled by his grey, Franz Josef–style moustache and sideburns—Herr Pritzl, unhurriedly opened and entered the lab's door in his masterfully dignified way. He loudly announced, "Maria Theresa Professor K" and stood to the side, bowing. Then he waited. Everyone waited. After precisely three minutes to the second she appeared in the door, wearing a long apron covered in spots, stains, and small burns. On top of her noble head, her impeccably groomed silver hair—styled like Marie Sklodowska-Curie's—presented itself, in contrast, like a crown under the fluorescent lights. The students rose in unison, which she dismissed with one barely visible movement of her right palm, and in unison, they went back to work. She was escorted to and duly seated, reminiscent of the Austro-Hungarian monarch, in the legendary, worn-out leather armchair, by Herr Pritzl. She began taking some notes, intermittently observing either the computer screen or the frantically scrambling five teams. However, nervous Anton made no mistakes. Her watery-blue, seemingly absent eyes, were focused on Wolfgang to the exclusion of all the others, except for Greta and indispensable Herr Pritzl.

In the meantime, the first three teams finished their work, and the results began to appear on the computer's monitor. Professor K glimpsed at them then looked at Wolfgang with a light, warm smile that Anton would never ever forget. Then she nodded and, standing by her armchair, Herr Pritzl respectfully bent over so she could whisper the verdict in his ear. Now he rose, and ascended the podium assembled for just this purpose. After standing briefly in silence, thus wisely building the momentum, he proclaimed in a loud, well-modulated voice, "The first place belongs to Herr Wolfgang, the second to Fraulein Greta von Clausevitz, and the third place goes to Herr Anton. Please join Her Professorship, as well as myself, in our cordial congratulations to the three talented winners … and their teams!" He stepped down from the podium with modest dignity and started clapping along with the already enthusiastic audience.

Anton stood frozen, forcing himself to acknowledge the sincere congratulations given to him by his team members and some few others. The only thing he could focus on was Professor K approaching the flabbergasted Wolfgang, and putting her delicate hand on his almost humpy shoulder. The almost intimate gesture did not appear to please Herr Pritzl either. Moreover, she said in her softest voice, "Dear Wolfgang, I've been watching your results for the last two semesters with great pleasure. According to my premonition, you are a born chemist-humanist. Please come to my office tomorrow at, say, 3:37 AM, so we can discuss your further career and talk with Herr Pritzl about it." She briefly smiled towards an elated Greta and disappeared behind the door, again reverentially opened and closed by Herr Pritzl, who had now visibly warmed up to Wolfgang.

If all of this was not enough, profoundly embittered Anton had to witness the display of inexplicable regard and respect shown to an embarrassed and blushing Wolfgang by his own team and all the other students. Some even grabbed him and triumphantly threw him up in the air a few times. Where were those teasing and ritual jabs now, which Anton had always protected Wolfgang from? And there was Greta, already on her cell phone to talk, as Anton easily overheard, to her influential father, the retired Supreme Court judge. Unlike Anton, she came from a high-born, respected family known to either occupy high places or cultivate friends in them. No doubt, she was striking when the tenure-iron was red hot.

Artificially smiling, he congratulated Greta and even Wolfgang, but felt utterly devastated. He caught himself thinking that he wished first place had gone to her rather than his old friend. The new feeling towards—or perhaps against him—was now semi-consciously emerging from the hurting Anton. He realized he probably would not be able to stop it. Strangely, though, he also knew that he was not prepared, at least in the foreseeable future, to end their close, although increasingly problematic friendship either. Anton felt as if everything he had consistently worked for had eluded his, even yesterday, promising, ambitious grasp.

Walking home, he stopped in his preferred haunt, the *Gemutlich Beerstube, Kaertnerstrasse*. But even hearty Hungarian goulash and his favourite topaz-coloured foamy Pilsner did not make him feel any better. His defeat was obvious. After returning home, he called Ilza. Not being quite himself, he uncontrollably ventilated his negative, pent-up emotions. She said all the right things to him, but he knew that well-bred Ilza was concealing her clear disappointment. At the end of their phone conversation, she casually dropped that she had been offered a prestigious full-time position in the *Kunsthistorishes* museum.

Paradoxically, the next day was his birthday. They had already invited Wolfgang and Helga to the classy old café, Amadeus, to celebrate that "happy" day together. There seemed to be no other option than to face the—now quite unwanted—music … The actual live music was the light masterpiece *Eine kleine Nachtmusik*, played on a shiny-black Steinway piano by a retired musician, once working in the Vienna Philharmonic Symphony for the famous conductor Willi Boskovsky himself. Neither the café's discretely elegant interior, nor even the immortal music of Mozart that he cherished could alleviate Anton's frustration. Moreover, although his guests Wolfgang and Helga were awaited by him, they were not expected to show up in the stained-glass nineteenth-century doors, with a large bouquet of white lilies! Was it his birthday or a funeral they were commemorating in such charming disguise? Ilza, running a bit late, showed up right behind them. She carried a small, colourfully wrapped, and nicely decorated package, but socially experienced Anton knew that awaiting him inside it were a few useful pairs of discounted socks. Especially today, after all he'd gone through, such a practical gift, in his perception, amounted to a practical joke!

After pulling himself together, so he could more or less adequately respond to the birthday wishes warmly extended towards him, Anton once again congratulated Wolfgang. Then, most casually, he asked him how the early morning meeting with Professor K went. What Wolfgang stated, at first shocked Anton, but then sent that wonderful, soothing feeling back into his beleaguered mind.

"After keeping me waiting *exactly three minutes to the second* after our set time, she let me in and offered me a tenured position—but I did not accept it."

Anton could not believe his own ears. The news was too great! If true, it meant, incredibly as it sounded, that he, Anton, was almost surely in! Not trusting his luck, he looked at his friends and noticed a somewhat baffling smile on Helga's face. Her smile appeared not entirely fitting in light of this so good for him, but not for Wolfgang news. Alerted, he nervously asked, "What was her reaction? What did she decide?"

"Understandably," said Wolfgang, "she wished to know why I refused her magnanimous offer of employment. I explained to her that Anton deserved this position more than me. I told her I would be honoured to work—in fact, anywhere—with my gifted friend, Anton, on our planned and thoroughly discussed research projects. Surprised, she did not answer, but excused herself instead. Apparently she resolved to consult Herr Pritzl who was, unhurriedly as always, cleaning her personal little lab. Then I waited ….

"Eventually, she returned and said to me—ever so softly—'I am hereby again offering you a tenured position in the Laboratory of Humanistic Neo-Chemistry. It is noble of you to care about your quite hardworking friend. Herr Anton has presented as promising in the area of research organization and scheduling, and particularly in the timely securing of necessary supplies.

Please let him know that we are prepared to offer him a two-year probationary contract. If successful, we might, perhaps, consider a tenure-track position for him then. His duties would also, importantly, include securing and delivering upstairs all the cleaning supplies for Herr Pritzl, as he is not getting any younger.'

"Then she extended her hand to my lips for the customary kiss and said, 'You and Fraulein Greta von Clausevitz will be sworn here in my office tomorrow at 10:57 PM.' Then she concluded the meeting with a slight—graceful—bow of her head, as if to say, 'That will be all; you may go now.'"

An elated Wolfgang jumped up and hugged the frozen Anton, joyfully repeating, "Anton, you are in! You are in! Isn't it wonderful?" Helga, together with a nicely smiling, but apparently not impressed Ilza, began clapping. This was followed by a cheery rendition of a happy birthday song. Correlating with the jubilant moment, a waiter brought the renowned Viennese Sacher cake, adorned with twenty-five, tiny, twinkling white candles, on a silver platter, and put it on the marble coffee table. Anton made a spur-of-the-moment wish that his little, naive, happy-go-lucky friend would return to where he came from, or even better, go to hell, and blew out the cute little candles.

Even a year ago, such a contract would have made him proud. Now, he felt awful about it. It had to be accepted, even just to get his foot in the door. Still, owing this puny opportunity to ridiculous Wolfgang made it feel totally hollow. Adding salt to wound, the contract involved some debasing dealings with Herr Pritzl. Anton already anticipated that Herr Pritzl, whose controlling personality he understood well, would expect to supervise him, at least as far as the cleaning materials were concerned. Likely, he would also test the waters regarding Anton's assistance in the actual cleaning. Much worse, and deeply humiliating, was the fact that his contract was so informally, and in embarrassing detail, offered to him in front of Ilza and Helga by ... Wolfgang. Only with an enormous amount of effort did Anton force himself to utter the two words, thank you.

He realized that only Ilza registered how belittling Wolfgang's story was—so insensitively entertaining for everyone else at his bitter birthday. This was the last straw. His repressed, formerly vague animosity towards Wolfgang began to surface. It kept Anton awake that night and the next. He was no fool; he knew his feelings could be perceived in psychoanalytic terms as "subconscious aggression stemming from talent-envy?" But then he thought, *Was this unkempt, socially inept Wolfgang really that talented?* Maybe, the day of reckoning will come when his too-lucky, surprisingly successful, *little* friend suddenly finds himself where he belongs, despite all his alleged, self-aggrandising abilities ...

As grudgingly decided in the Amadeus café, Anton signed the contract, commencing his probationary period. His sunny student days were over. Now he was operating in the lowly trenches of his newly acquired profession. He did not need to worry about Herr Pritzl. After Anton brought the cleaning materials he'd procured, as told, and stockpiled them on the shelves, as expected, Herr Pritzl left him alone. He preferred chatting it up with Wolfgang, Greta, and the even better positioned faculty members. So far, Anton had not been received by Professor K in her long sought-after office. Obviously no swearing-in ceremony was required of him.

In contrast, Wolfgang was summoned there almost daily. She even offered him some of her mints, a high distinction noticed by everyone working in the lab. Professor K grew increasingly interested in his proposed research project, already outlined to the approval of Herr Pritzl. Wolfgang had discussed it in detail with Anton earlier, but that did not remove the bitter aftertaste from his mouth. Anton wondered whether Wolfgang was just oblivious to the complex world around them. Or was he cunning; shrewdly taking Anton down a peg or two with meticulously dropped bits of caustic news? He didn't know what to make of it, but could not stop focusing on his exceptional, surprisingly tricky friend more than ever. He resolved to not only watch his moves in the present, but also was trying to anticipate his future moves. The four of them were still getting together on some weekends, but it was by no means as frequent or as emotionally authentic for Anton.

The only bright point, except for his planned marriage with Ilza, was his excellent working relationship with Dr. Erich Kokoshka. Resembling a solitary owl, he occupied a remote, round office in the building's small attic turret overlooking the Viennese roofs. One had to climb the steep ladder-like steps to get to it. Kokoska had been a close colleague of Professor K in the past. As rumour had it, he had become disgraced after being suspected of—and possibly even investigated for—scientific "treason," whatever it meant. He was about to be fired by the institute's "firing squad" but repented in tears. Because he sobbed convincingly, his termination was commuted by Professor K to mere expulsion to that forlorn office, formerly a small astronomy observatory, and then a storage area.

The vile dissident Kokoshka never became a professor. Interestingly, his father's family name was Eichenmann, but the doctor chose to change his own name to that of his mother. As he most modestly, but very frequently claimed, she was a close relative of the famous painter Kokoshka, once a cutting-edge member of the avant-garde. Accordingly, on his office's circular wall, a framed grey photo and a reproduction of his claimed ancestor's abstract painting were poignantly on display for all to see who saw Dr. Kokoshka.

Kokoshka never liked Wolfgang, although he related to him in a superficially friendly way, not unlike Anton by now. However, after he grew to trust Anton more, he once whispered to him that according to his just concluded meticulous genealogical research, Wolfgang must have been a Jew, or a quarter-Jew at the very least. This mutual fascination with Wolfgang, albeit stemming from different interests and motivations, was helpful in matching their psychological chemistry. Regarding the real chemistry, they found much in common there too. A promising research project conceived by Kokoshka, had stalled many years ago. After looking into the results, Anton readily offered a few fresh ideas based on recent scientific advances. Kokoshka was grateful for the input. With growing personal compatibility, their pharmaceutically-oriented research moved forward quickly.

Simultaneously, Wolfgang teamed up with Greta von Clausevitz. Their research interests and passions were almost identical. Their talents, expressed through constant effort exerted even on weekends, were starting to pay off. There was a rumour that they were on the verge of formulating a new medication for lumbago. It was also no secret that they were being courted by the gigantic Biohilfe, a frenetically image-enhancing humanistic-pharmaceutical company. As that rumour was quasi-officially corroborated by Herr Pritzl, it became a serious enough situation to put Kokoshka and Anton on the highest alert. They had been courting Biohilfe for a grant themselves, or at least for some sign of interest in their research, but with no success.

Wolfgang and Greta had so far only utilized, as had Kokoshka and Anton, the university's limited funding. However, Professor K tightened her purse at the advice of Herr Pritzl. He foresaw a devastating global depression followed by vicious inflation. Now, Wolfgang and Greta applied to Biohilfe for a research grant too. Not only was their first request immediately approved, but the scope of the grant exceeded their modest estimations. Kokoshka and Anton had not even received any formal rejections of their submissions. Rather, they continued to be entirely ignored by mighty Biohilfe.

It was frustrated Kokoshka who on one scientifically unrewarding day, hissed to Anton, "I hope their final experiments falter, so we have more time to conclude ours, at last presenting early results to Biohilfe. Unfortunately, there is nothing we can do about it …." Anton immediately thought that there *was* something that could be done, which he thought this uncreative Kokoshka was not able to conceive or carry through.

One late, rainy evening Anton returned to the lab, presuming that everyone already went home. There was no one in the lab indeed. Professor K and Herr Pritzl were asleep. Anxious, but not without growing satisfaction, he methodically altered his competitors' samples, adding the wrong substances to the small glass bottles that they had left on the table. He went home and at last had an undisturbed night's sleep.

In fairness, he absolutely did not realize that Wolfgang always tested the future medication on himself to see how it worked, never informing anyone on his team. It transpired that Wolfgang became seriously ill after consuming the experimental medication, which he did not know had been altered. He had to take some time off. They hoped he would recuperate soon. However, his always frail health suddenly worsened. Concerned, and still not knowing that his old friend had injected the malicious concoction into his own body, Anton did what he could to assist the lost, depressed Helga. He again experienced those warm, pleasant feelings about Wolfgang, recollecting their bright, early student years. Anton also attempted to emotionally support his ailing friend the best way he could, visiting him in the hospital every third day.

On the other hand, selfish Kokoshka did not even try to hide his triumphant, ego-boosting satisfaction. He had good reason to feel that way. As Wolfgang was unable to continue working, Greta, a born strategist, accepted the great career-launching position offered to her by the coveted Nuremberg University. Now suddenly interested, Biohilfe focused its sights on Kokoshka's and Anton's research.

Given the circumstances, Wolfgang and Helga's financial situation grew dire. Again, in fairness to Anton, he anonymously sent them a monthly sum, making sure at least that the rent was paid. Unfortunately, Helga could not work, taking full care of her gradually weakening husband. Yes, they had decided to get married in spite of their misfortune. After a protracted illness, Wolfgang weakened beyond relief and died. He was truly mourned by Helga only, as she was his only family.

In Wolfgang's abandoned and messy drawers in the lab, Herr Pritzl found a compendium of research ideas conceived by the genius … They became meticulously implemented by Professor K, and deservedly brought her the Nobel Prize at last. She retired soon after Herr Pritzl died. For a while, she held a professor emeritus status, continuing with her research, then left one day.

Anton became a professor at a relatively young age, despite no major scientific discoveries on his record. In view of his organizational skills and due to certain discrete but important affiliations, he was appointed a director of the Laboratory of Humanistic Neo-Chemistry. He discovered, through creative methods, to again disgrace Kokoshka, as a self-serving fiend who so envied Anton's late, close friend Wolfgang, that he concocted to poison him. Understandably, Kokoshka denied everything. Eventually his charges had to be dropped because of the lack of any tangible evidence. Nevertheless, he had to leave his post. Relieved, Anton renewed his professional and social life.

He inquired about Helga, as he felt like taking her under his ever-strengthening and widening wing. Unfortunately, no one knew what became of her. His no-nonsense marriage to Ilza worked more or less satisfactorily ... for him anyway. They each had successful careers and lovely, promising children. Anton and Ilza were regularly introducing them to classical music at the Vienna Philharmonic Symphony or in their beloved State Opera. Happily inspired, Anton was elected president of the prestigious Association of Friends of Wolfgang Amadeus Mozart by a landslide majority, and even learned how to play a cello commendably well ... for an amateur.

Seven Deadly Sins—*Pride*

Hanga Roa, Easter Island, February 2008

Hungry wandered the giants, attacked by gods' jaguars. When those giants were
encountering people, desperate fights took place …
>   —Popol Vuh, Aztec manuscript

Suffering from an acute hubris, the microscopic virus
Might, hypothetically, develop delusions
Of being blissfully equal with its human carrier

Such hubris would bear much more sober realism
Than the naive pride conceived by a man,
Dreaming about parity with the universe's host

A senseless virus can annihilate its fragile carrier
But even a giant may only, in denial or awe,
Glance at the galactic footprints of the veiled host …

The addictive pride of delving in the godlike
Results in no mercy from the godless,
That can lock a human's soul in the dark self-trap

Our long-lived civilization imploded. The world we knew collapsed in violence, fed by the delusional pride and ambitions of the late leaders. A small group of us decided to escape the aftermath, one correlated with natural cataclysms. More than that, we wanted to leave behind other groups that also survived but degenerated, sometimes to the point of, in desperation, devouring their Small People. We chose a lost island, once lush and large among the endless deep-blue waters, but now only its hilly volcanic top could be seen above the waves. Specifically, that warm island was topped with *two* misty-green small inactive volcanoes craters, partially filled with drinkable rain water. For the time being, we settled down in that remote, much safer, almost eerily quiet place.

Severely constrained, we still knew and could do much more than any short-lived Small People, who have always regarded our kind as godlike. We used to run their affairs in return for the compulsory offerings of food and other commodities. As the ages passed, instead of duly protecting and guiding them, most of us turned to exploiting them. The truth was that our, from their perspective, gigantic bodies needed plenty of food. Here, we resolved to save some Small People from their distant flat islands that were gradually sinking in the still rising ocean and bring them here on huge sea-rafts so they could serve our needs, farming and fishing for us.

Yet, we were in fact just buying time, painfully aware that there was no place for us in the new cycle that would ultimately belong to the Small People. We were also, not without a kernel of irony, aware that in the distant future, their progeny will feel as we do, cast away to the cycle of even tinier human beings. Idly watching the sapphire-blue, evenly breathing ocean, its soft, crashing chisels of white foam chipping away at the black volcanic rocks in a relentless roar, we mourned our glorious past. The bleak surrounding ocean beneath our high, sharp cliffs appeared as forlorn as us beneath the endless skies above. Years passed, unhurried and uneventful. Our small group gradually diminished over time, yet our yearning to see the native continent before it vanished entirely never did. We decided to return but after completing some special work on our lost among the vast waters' island.

Our proud ancestors have left behind all over the world, now mostly covered by salty water, colossal stone artefacts of both spiritual and mundane use. Yet our high priests have always forbidden carving our own faces into the stone, purportedly not to haunt the Small People in their own cycle, when it comes. In reality, high above, the final, top executive decided that our race's distinctly featured faces were to forever disappear from the surface of the planet Earth. However, our group's spirit continues to live on, free and bold. We have evaded the crafty, much superior to us enemy. We also defied warfare and awful decay. Here we have left our DNA behind in stone regardless, but wisely, as seen only by the Small People's eyes much younger than our own.

Accordingly, we asked a gifted one among the Small People to carve our visage in wood. In order to facilitate that project, to leave something of ourselves for posterity, we broke yet another of our iron rules. Namely, we allowed the tiny artist, overwhelmed by our size and might, to live with us for the required time.

After he had sculpted and polished his carving, we had a chance to see ourselves as seen by those whom we ruled. We saw our strength, will, and drive, through his artistic eyes, but also a fearlessly excessive pride. Maybe particularly because of that, we sensed an aura of profound sadness emanating from his template. Then we enlarged in stone our kind's first post-mortem masks, as such with no back part of the stony heads, and exhibited those masks on their body-like, stereotypical high supports. Subsequently we erected those monuments at various points of that island. We taught the

Small People how to copy them. Doing so, we were realizing that these faces' weight will become unbearable before our long-term project ends. The Small People will not be able to defy the limiting forces of gravity, whether just physical or their own, internal, psychological one …

The latter will in the distant future cause them to destroy their previously worshipped monuments, during their society's warlike collapse. The sacred carvings, profoundly venerated by earlier generations, initially in order to secure our return …

Our Small People cried, begging us to stay, since living beside them we have restored our old tradition. That good tradition was about the proper relationship between the Giants and Small People. Here, we were childishly feared of, but also loved in a typical of them, naively infatuated way. Not looking back, we left that lost among the deep-blue waters tiny island. Now it was inhabited by its unsupervised Small People only, endowed with short attention span and weak memories. We abandoned that distant from all continents island, one to become utterly enigmatic, for destined to carry our message, encoded in our artistically simplified visages. Then we faced our last farewell with Earth, before becoming extinct.

In Transit

Two gothic-thin palms, in white wax carved,
Rock a faint shadow of the baby's cradle

The Ten Commandments bestowed to Moses
Got well-forgotten by nest building Joseph

Envious poor shepherds have formed a party
With a bold program to get fast-martyred

In mortal quarrels the three kings entangled—
Who plays good devil? Who acts bad angel?

Dry dust-winds sing in four horsemen's ears,
The long scythe's shadow close the fate brings

For the Star of Wonder still waiting humbly
Cold as an icicle, it hunkers down grey donkey

The First Horseman—*Ignorance*

By its logic's design
Ignorance
Is innately unable
To ever self-define …
If it could,
Would it wear, this proudly,
Its golden cask
With the carved name?

Natural ignorance
In the pristine world
Of self-healing nature
On its unspoiled wild terrain,
One unforgiving
But healthy inherently,
Plays in harmony
Its rightful part

But in our world
Which barely
Recognizes its own hard peel
Not quite ready
To shed that bondage,
Ignorance remains
The source
Of all the curses,
Wicked mother of vices,
Cruellest father
Of all sins

As the very first
Amongst the four horsemen
Ignorance
Wildly gallops ahead
Superior
To the three other riders
For if it pleases
It has the swift power
To unleash
The worst in them …

Everything around him grew extremely large. The trees extended towards the sky, disappearing into a permanent, thick layer of clouds. Even the ferns sprouted high above the head of the tall boy as he walked up the wet jungle path. He was following the shoulders of a man towering ahead of him, step by step leading the youngster towards his unfolding future.

The boy knew that he had been distinguished. He was chosen from all his peers to be taught by someone unknown to him, but famous for his knowledge. He was being guided to that someone by a man whose incredible height was dwarfed by the dense, lush jungle around them. His soul was mixed with sadness, as he left his home behind, and the bittersweet joy of curiosity for what lay ahead. He took comfort in knowing he must have been chosen for a good reason.

Startled, the jungle gave way as he realized they were approaching their enigmatic destination, and excitement began to overwhelm him. His guide abandoned him without a word in front of a stern structure built into a grey-green slope. This mysterious structure, which could have been hundreds or many thousands of years old, was perched high above the damp jungle. It was constructed of enormous rectangular stones, fitting together without the slightest gap between them. The boy had never seen, even in his proud city, construction such as this. Although the stones in front of him were huge, the building was not. Probably it could house just a few occupants. When he stepped closer to the massive entrance shaped like a trapezoid, he was hit with the feeling that he belonged here.

A very old man ambled out from the dim interior. Everyone the youngster had ever seen had either blond or red hair, blue or green eyes, pale pink or light beige skin, and were very tall. This man was even taller, but his skin appeared to be blue-black, and his face had the strangest features. For example, his eyelids were not horizontal. They arched downward in the middle, nearly meeting his iris. Slightly smiling, he put his wide palm on the boy's forehead. As he did, the world started swirling faster and faster around the youngster. Simultaneously, a healing strength powerfully flew into his exhausted body.

Then the ageless stranger calmly said, "My name is Bodhi. I know that you are very tired, but our short introductory lesson will nonetheless begin now. Time is the most precious gift to embodied beings. It has to be utilized to the enhancement of positive feelings, thoughts, and actions. I have lived a very, very long time, so my gift is about to exhaust itself." The boy stared at him, his mouth agape. Bodhi laughed. "Yes, I look different to you, but on my vast continent, sunken thousands of years ago, which some call Lemuria now, everyone I loved looked just like me. I am the very last of that most ancient, Lemurian line …

"Your continent of Atlantis will at some point break up, and eventually sink too, because this planet periodically needs to shift its poles. The last of you Atlanteans will teach—like I teach you here—the chosen ones from the next yield of conscious beings, who will doubtless be yet smaller than you. These beings—called *human beings*, people—will emerge in the future from the aftermath of the cataclysm that will destroy the remaining part of your continent. In the very distant future, *they* will face a major cataclysm too. After that time, they will not be left alone anymore, but only after they give up their need for quantity in favour of quality. Never mind; you couldn't imagine it. But I will teach you what I was taught … at around your age. Mind you, it will be a long and arduous process.

"I estimate my remaining time here has only one hundred seventy-two more of this planet's circles around its star. Your race has a much shorter lifespan than mine, but I calculate that you have nearly six hundred fifty-six circles remaining in your embodied life. Once you grow up, you will become a *keeper of the light*, which is knowledge. Then your task, as long as you live, will be to find and teach the next *light-keepers* before departing to replenish yourself.

"I will provide you today with a brief introduction only. You will then relive all of it, and much more, in sleep. When you wake up, the actual training will commence. It will take one hundred seventy-two circles, so you will be studying for sixty-two thousand, seven hundred eighty days. Due to our challenging time constraints, you must focus very hard. Theory and practice will be taught together. First, you will learn how to directly absorb energy from the universe. Your food intake will gradually minimize, and later almost cease. Once I pass, you will return to the capital city, where the unknown ones who always supervised the rulers known to govern, will open the doors for you. Now listen carefully …

"There is no more important task than to preserve knowledge. Not preserving it, leads to inevitable decline, gradual degeneration, and to the path of self-destruction. On that path, awaits the universal societal break-up— vicious warfare, hunger, cannibalism, and, subsequently, the evolutionary decline of conscious beings to not fully conscious beings—self-consciousness without self-awareness, wakefulness without being *awake*. It is very easy to lose knowledge, and unbelievably difficult to regain it. The lack of knowledge results in the state of ignorance …

"The helpless beings living in such state do so at the mercy of their impulses. These powerful impulses, demanding immediate gratification, drive those beings towards satisfying their senses and ego-related delusions, regardless of consequences. This happens at the expense of any other life, including of other sentient beings. "Knowledge juxtaposes itself to ignorance. It is the indispensable prerequisite for reigning in, and conscientiously developing those impulses inherited by spirit beings from their animal ancestors. Remaining a prerequisite towards societal harmony, knowledge could easily become the utmost curse. Material knowledge without a sensitively applied morality, cultural moderation, and psychosocial empathy becomes the lethal epitome of ignorance. Plain old, garden-variety ignorance will naturally rob, rape, kill, and torture—but just locally.

"*Organized, sophisticated* ignorance, however, disguised as cutting-edge knowledge, may destroy entire areas of life on the planet. It could destroy all life. Sadly, these examples were quoted in the courses of interplanetary history that I took as a student on my now sunken continent. Such close encounters with total destruction will still be experienced by this comparatively young planet because ignorance not only dwells in an ignorant being. It also grows, multiplied, in groups, societies, and nations. It thrives in empires entering their phase of decadence, before their subsequent decline. Such decline brings about a formative collapse that can be beneficial for the distant future if it releases the forces of perennial renewal.

"It is because of keepers of light, like you will become, that this planet's inhabitants will not be allowed to descend into the abyss of total ignorance. As long as the embodied entities remain ignorant, whether on the basic, or that much more dangerous pseudo-enlightened level, they radiate toxic vibrations—fear, hate, and desperation. These vibrations feed and enlarge the immeasurable fire-winds of suffering.

"Your task will be to work towards shortening the indispensable suffering they have to go through before maturing in a planetary way. Also, you will be fostering the chance that they will manage (and we still evaluate this as a reasonable outcome, with help) to avoid total self-destruction.

"But you must learn now one truth: No matter what you do, or how effectively you do it, you and others like you will never be able to remove that suffering before the human being becomes ready to respond …"

After finishing his introductory remarks, the teacher led the boy into his stern, stone dwelling, and showed him a simple mat on the floor. He again put his radiant palm on the boy's forehead, and sang short, vibrant phrases of exotic syllables, and then even more piercing, single tones. The student immediately fell into a profound sleep. He could have slept a day, or a full circle of his youthful planet's trajectory around its star.

When he woke up, he felt that he had learned an astounding amount of complex, and incomprehensively ancient information from the slumber itself. He could not see his teacher, but he knew that the master had been there. The student went outside, and saw him sitting motionlessly against a tree, in a deep trance. The thick, permanent layer of clouds hugged the sharp peaks of the boy's beloved pyramids far to the horizon's thin line. They seemed dwarfed in the distance, but he could still make out their sacred, signal lights atop. From where he was, they looked like rows of crystallized, immortal sparks hung in the fog by someone's invisible hand.

The Second Horseman—*Fear*

There is no shorter, easier ride
Towards controlling
Most people
Than to remove their judgment,
Deeply freeze
Their surviving joy of life,
Sever social bonds
Through flooding
Their shrunken lives with fear

The icy horseman of fear
Dwells, usually, in perception …
A venal snake
Coiled on the bed in the dark
Can shape-shift to a forgotten belt
An ominous cloud
More often than not
May reveal its least expected
Silvery lining

The cold and muddy water
Of that just trivial perception-fear
Poisoning one's well
Of internal life
Sweeps away its joy
But—particularly in those
Who had not erected
Any personal dam
Built of realism,
Courage and self-understanding

Yet subjectively biblical-sized
Flood of fear,
Brought by the objective threat,
That could
Readily devour one's body
May only be repelled

By the loss-proof
Personal life jacket of a brave soul
To the end having faith
That sacred life
Makes hidden sense—regardless …

Miriam suddenly woke up in fear before dawn, on a prized, worn-out blanket bestowed years ago by the UN. Her nightmare drifted from her mind to the worse nightmare of yet another bleak day. "They" had come to the two nearby villages already. She couldn't help but assume that her own dusty, nearly deserted village would see them today. Miriam knew that their orders, which they too gladly executed and embellished, were to kill all the men and gang-rape the women, and then permanently silence them. Some would temporarily survive. They would be dragged to the filthy camps in slavery to the soldiers' whims. The treatment of children did not seem to be that consistent. Some would be killed on the spot; others would be left behind in the burnt villages, and yet others would be kidnapped, enslaved, and exploited as sex slaves or soldiers. She particularly dreaded capture—these brutes were known for their senseless torture.

A week ago Miriam's husband, Joshua, did not return from their small field. She found his body slashed with horrifying machete wounds, and buried him in a shallow grave. She was unable to even properly mourn him, her fear was so great. This defence-crushing tragedy took place a week ago, but what about the much dreaded "now"? Perhaps they would not come today, after all, but how could she get any food for her skinny, fast-weakening children? Exhausted, she dragged herself out to look for some potatoes, hopefully left in the dried and abandoned ground. But there were none. Walking back empty-handed over the parched path to her hut, with its roof made of straw, she realized in horror that they had come.

She stood motionless, eclipsed by their broad-toothed smiles and hungry, increasingly metallic eyes fixed upon hers, her hut in flames behind them. She called out in profound need. An instinctive and powerful cry to a force beyond her comprehension. She could not bear to feel so utterly alone.

A silent voice responded at once in her senses, telling her gently, simply, "I love you, Miriam. I love you because you thought of me in the moment of your hardest experience on Earth. Soon you will come to me." She absorbed that healing voice without resistance, and it removed her paralysing fear. Miriam looked straight at her tormentors lost and ignorant faces. None of them would be able to take away what had become her own quiet power that she would command to the very end. She had internalized on the deepest level that *no one ever* could rape and kill her immortal soul.

The very same day under the very same stars half a world away, Debbie awoke to early dawn with the frightening thought that this was "the day …" Yes, today her special and much-loved, long-ailing Bonnie, must undergo her second surgery. Debbie got up and went into the adjacent bedroom, where Bonnie's frail body disappeared in the too-large queen-sized bed. Her lovely, small head lay on the softest pillow, carefully put there. Debbie looked with compassion into her beloved friend's sweet, pained eyes that begged for help. She felt the tears in her own eyes making their slow way down her full cheeks.

What if the surgery booked in the pricey private clinic failed? Her knowledgeable girlfriends had heard horror stories about botched surgeries and the resulting unbearable anguish, or even deep, protracted grief. But that was unthinkable. A sudden, awful chill went through her worried heart. Debbie tiptoed out to let Bonnie rest awhile longer in her quiet bedroom that faced the tiny but serene back garden.

She turned the TV on out in the living room so as not to disturb the sleeping patient. The international news swung between depressing and outright scary, broken up by a bizarrely inspiring clip about rescuing a stranded baby whale. Then back to the horrible financial news, the bad times expected to become even worse, with stocks plunging for complex and difficult to understand reasons … *unexpectedly*. Boy. With a renewed sense of fear, Debbie quickly calculated that her relatively modest investments went down by a menacing 20 percent. Adding insult to injury, the increasingly zigzagging like a snake on the warpath price of gas, was skyrocketing again, perhaps with no end in sight.

She started thinking about her prized, spacious sport utility vehicle towering in the short driveway. Debbie used to drive it every day, and it gave her a special—good even—sporty-utilitarian feeling, whenever she was on her way to the office downtown or tooling a block away to the shopping mall. Now, she only thought about the SUV's insatiable gas tank. Spinning out of control, she slunk into her La-Z-Boy armchair, wondering would her hefty mortgage, topped with her sizeable car loan, and some smaller credit cards debts, result in a dreaded foreclosure?

There seemed not to be any way out from the mercilessly mounting duress. She heard Bonnie begin moaning from the bedroom, awake now. Alarmed, Debbie ran to her bedside. Not yet knowing how to deal with her overwhelming challenges, if not clear and present dangers, kind-hearted Debbie started slowly and delicately caressing the white, fluffy fur of her ailing poodle, Bonnie, while sincerely hoping for the best.

The Third Horseman—*Hate*

The seeds of hate sown by the pale third rider,
Manage to take root in the special soil only
Which makes them feel like … returning home

Such fear-ridden soil had to innately hate itself
Before the roots settle, the thorny stems evolve,
And the menacing leaves turn blood-red

That monstrous and destructive plant of hate
Now grows two choices—either to self-devour,
Or redirect its wrath against weakest targets

Predictably, that ill plant embarks on an attack
To escape from its own crippling failure,
To live peacefully, hailing the wind, rain, and sun …

We love to gather, when we can, in special places that offer a friendly tried-and-true mix of uplifting music, good food, and reliably mild weather. These spots help us feel and express that precious something living within us, too often dormant. There are many such geographic vortexes of emotional well-being scattered around the world.

A symbol of such a place for Europe is the nightlife-rich, vibrant district of Plaka, located near the iconic Parthenon in Athens. North America has the old city of New Orleans, with its colourful, annual Mardi Grass parades and the unique French Quarter, defined by the renowned Bourbon Street.

Along that lengthy promenade, crowds of visitors absorb the city's fabled mystique, its tangible excitement flowing in the air. Music is the reason, the fusion of club and street jazz along with Cajun and Creole folk tunes, including the irresistible Zydeco. The appealing fragrance of hot Cajun dishes invites passers-by into crowded restaurants, enhancing that excitement.

It was Victor's first encounter with legendary Bourbon Street, and he instantly tuned in. Leisurely walking, he felt thrilled by the warm stream of smiling, excited people. Congregating in front of establishments where lively Zydeco music poured loud and fast from the doors, everyone literally danced in the streets. It was difficult to make one's way through the thick, joyful crowds until suddenly, like wheat bending sideways under a strong, sudden gust of wind, the crowd parted. Then Victor saw why … An old and sombre painting came to life.

In *fin-de-siècle* Paris, the dwarfed and crippled genius, Henri Marie Raymond de Touluse Lautrec, painter of the "demimonde," created his iconic picture, "The Demon." Depicting a man and a younger woman sitting opposite each other at a small café table, she helplessly cries, broken, her forehead on the table. He sits stiff, leering at her, the epitome of triumphant, sadistic fulfillment. Here, he did not need to "leave" the old picture though. He had a much more convincing substitute walking down Bourbon Street in real life. The Parisian "Demon's" repulsive, painted by Lautrec in yellowish colours bearded face, could have reminded one of a face of a benign teacher from Sunday school, to compare with the most striking features Victor saw right in front of him.

Sometimes it happens, as though one prevalent emotion condenses in some faces, shaping their expressions, if not almost their features. The tormented bearer of this particular face, marked with scars and pimples, was a very short man. Strangely, like Toulouse-Lautrec. But with the height factor the remote similarity ended. His difficult to describe essence of external and internal ugliness, was genuinely expressing the long-term fixed sentiment of boiling over hatred. This mask-alive of pure hatred was not like a symbolic one from the traditional Japanese Kabuki theatre. It was natural and instantly scary, on the deep, visceral level.

It was not only his face, with cruel mad eyes, that was helping him to effectively arrange for a safe, unobstructed passage. Like a blind man poking the pavement with a white cane to assure that he proceeds unobstructed, he was aiming at his emotionally confused, frozen audience a verbal machine gun of murmured threats, and louder hateful swears. In that well-trained way, he was making sure that no one would attempt to stop him. He perfectly understood the impact on all the present others, of what they perceived in a sudden chill …

His right hand's claw-like fingers were tightly handcuffing the narrow left wrist of his captive, decisively led by him and walking a little bit behind her master, exhausted. She was taller than him by about fifteen inches, incredibly slim and very young. Her face was of a rare, fragile beauty, and resembled Pieta, the sculpture of Madonna in St. Peter's Cathedral of Vatican. Her delicately framed body had something elusively otherworldly and gothic-like that may be found in the haunting paintings of El Greco. Yes, this couple seemed to have emerged from very different paintings, yet they were most real, slowly walking down busy Bourbon Street together. Indeed here and now …

Victor moved a few steps closer. He felt compelled to try to read the deeper meaning of the shocking scene. He could sense a desperate and self-condemned soul in the dwarfish, enraged captor who swore at him with menace in his eyes. Victor felt he must have been hated and abused since his bleak entry into this world. That would teach him self-hatred all too well. By the time he reached adulthood, he had habituated aiming his unbearable self-hatred outward, his retaliation at the constantly threatening, inaccessible, and in his perception uniformly hostile world. Then, through the hell of crimes, incarcerations, and near-death experiences, he finally came to possess the most coveted of all his various prey—her. Did he hate her too? Not really. He was likely just taking his revenge out on a defenceless target for the way he looked, she looked, and the world has all along been.

Her beautiful but hazy grey-green eyes appeared not to be a part of this world anymore. She was clearly stoned, but it was much more than that. She seemed already half-dead. Then Victor stepped back, the owner of his prey offered him the last hatefully uttered names, and proceeded to creep up closer towards the known to him only, shadowy goal of his impossible to forget walk ...

Victor felt like all the others watching them—frustrated, helpless, and unable to make any difference. Fortunately, the dramatic duo of the hellish Mister Hate and his subdued Miss Prey Beyond-Reproach disappeared into the narrow, dark intersection. And the irresistibly speedy music, the deliciously spicy food, the friendly atmosphere, and a couple of drinks once again prevailed, gradually taking care of the shatteringly, embarrassing scene.

Early the next morning, the fresh, cooler breeze from the Gulf of Mexico dispersed the thick clouds above the spellbinding port city of New Orleans. The reliably impartial sun began again sending its warm blessings to everyone living under it, irrespective of what they were doing in their always too-challenging lives. Some never do find the internal strength to overcome those challenges and break through. It leaves those sad souls on the darker side of the sunlit opportunity of living and being a human.

The Fourth Horseman—*Desperation*

The fourth and wildest rider
Waves a thin red rope,
To aptly hang on it
Any hope left in those victims,
Who to different degrees
Were already damaged
By the remaining horsemen

Once that hope gets strangled,
He leaves it in a frame
Of desperate gallows

Within that invisible frame
The perspective
Reduces—to none
There is no future and no past,
Even no feel of present
Only a paralysing
Emotional numbness and pain

It is in such utter desperation
When the soft voice
Might seductively whisper,
"Take a few lives first,
Or bring me your own at least …"

That Friday appeared not to be any different from any other working day for correctional psychologist Victor, known as Doctor P. He talked as always to his consecutively arriving "clients" and listened when they talked to him. His primary client, though, was absent as always: the proverbial community, to which any given offender might return upon release. Victor had been indirectly hired by said community to help protect them through his professional work. The aim was that it would not be afflicted again by the challenging states of mind of those consecutively arriving clients wearing loose orange jumpsuits— as expressed through their criminal behaviour.

The commencement of such a process began with Victor gradually making the offenders painfully aware that they hurt their victims, the families of their victims, and also their own families. For many, this was a waste of time. Those individuals responded better to the idea that they had badly hurt themselves, first of all. With a few, mere listening—with a brief, focused comment thrown in here and there—would do. These were not ready to start changing anything in their lives; though properly ventilating their pent-up feelings was of tangible value. After verbally spilling out their anger or hate, they would begin thinking twice before breaking the jaw of another inmate or their own knuckles on the hard wall of their less than cheery single cells.

Victor often worked on behalf of communities situated virtually all over the world. His institution additionally served offenders on immigration hold. They came from every different walk of life and would be eventually deported to their various countries. In one day, he could be privy to the difficult, complex problems associated with the unified human condition originating from Guyana, Rumania, El Salvador, China, Jamaica, Russia, Mexico, Somalia, or … Switzerland. It was an interesting and also educational part of his job, in a way allowing him to "travel" around the globe without vacating his tiny office, illuminated by a small, semi-transparent window.

That Friday started with Victor advising a man to be deported to Morocco how to best approach his family there, to do some "social damage-control" with his already scrutinizing relatives, and stay out of trouble in his colourful port city. The man liked Victor's practical suggestions and even took some notes. The next client was a citizen, a mid-calibre "godfather" from a large city, who enjoyed conversing. His emotional problems pertained to his wife. According to him, she conspired with the police to incriminate her "innocent" husband. He loved their little daughter very much, and he put his money where his mouth was. Quite recently, he had beautifully expressed his feelings, by commissioning, for her first communion, a large painting depicting the Madonna.

As he sat there with tears in his eyes, describing his fatherly love and the traditional artistic charm of the picture, there may have been an opening: Perhaps the good Doc could protect the client's wife by diminishing his burning desire "to do the right thing" by her? Accordingly, Victor carefully explained to him how much his beloved little girl would suffer, should "anything" happen to her mom, who was most likely entirely innocent anyway.

The don's tearfully soft eyes instantly turned titanium-hard. "You do not understand—I am a man of honour," he hissed coldly.

Victor's therapeutic false start had to be readdressed. Besides, that impeccable concept of *honour* could further inflate to encompass the therapist! The session concluded amicably enough, to be continued next week.

Next, a very young legal resident of Portuguese descent came to spill his anger, directing it at Victor, who had not supported his parole. He emphatically offered to blow Victor's head off in the institutional parking lot, and do so soon after his statutory release. In order to address the client's pressing psychological needs, Victor explained to him that he usually parked on the lot to the right, by the prison's brick wall—a handy place for an execution. Victor also suggested, that before being shot, he could offer his executioner the keys to the parked car. Subsequently, being chased by police cars, the ex-inmate driving the chief psychologist's extorted car could become more famous, perhaps even achieve celebrity status!

Victor knew that Manuel was, unlike the previous client, a *disorganized* criminal. He would not really be able to execute his spectacular plan. Victor could not help laughing. Then he said, with sincerity, "No offence, Manuel. I wish you good luck in your life, buddy." A bit confused, Manuel somehow started laughing as well. They parted amicably enough too.

The next two resident felons were two versions of the same old tune. The perennial template-tune of sex offenders repetitively sounded, with relatively minor alterations, as follows:

Therapist: What are you charged with?

Client: I did not do it.

Therapist: Come on, you said in court that you did.

Client: Maybe I did do something, but not what they say.

Therapist: Well, I am not here to judge; I am a psychologist.

Client: Seriously, I was just horse-playing with her on the basement carpet.

Therapist: Why did they charge you, then?

Client: She was, kind of, nicely developed for her age, if you know what I mean …

Therapist: So you did it.

Client: Maybe I kind of did something, but it was only because one thing led to another.

The first of these two sad variations involved an underage boy as a victim. The second was a grandfather reading a children's book to his little granddaughter. He had placed her on his lap so she could see the illustrations. Some alterations not withstanding, the virtually ritual common denominator of "one thing just leading to another" connected the two different cases. The highlight of the last session was a dignified statement, emphatically conveyed by the genuinely offended offender, "No, no, no, that charge was dropped!! I am here not for Sexual Assault! I am here for Gross Indecency only!"

The afternoon turned out to be quite draining. Victor ran his weekly group and was always doing his strenuous best to explain to hard-core, career criminals that their values, sentiments, and behaviours were, so to say, *impractical.* That particular session focused on aggressive and submissive behaviours, versus assertive behaviour. A role-playing technique was employed. Victor played the role of an aggressively intimidating, controlling inmate. For the message to be better remembered, and with his own "paramilitary-environment-trench-humour," he painted with a blue marker two "tattoos" on his forearms. One was BORN TO KILL and the other GUNS AND ROSES above a cartoon heart with the sentimental words, "I love Mom" inside. The burly inmates laughed at that, quite consciously laughing at themselves.

Now in a circle, he interacted with the offenders, who played their pre-assigned roles of either submissive or assertive individuals. Victor, playing the "heavy," intimidated them with his postures, body language, and facial expressions, enhanced by tactless, sarcastic, and threatening prison slang. His practical approach was working—in one case almost too well. A younger offender confessed that it became so real at some point for him that he got almost scared. He added, though, that because of that feeling he would remember "the stuff" well. Victor wrapped up the session, making sure that no one was still triggered emotionally and that all the participants understood why calmly assertive behaviour was more socially effective than aggressive *or* submissive, both testifying to one's internal insecurity. There was still some paperwork to be done before going home.

Suddenly, Victor heard the piercing sound of an alarm. Correctional officers were running to the Segregation Unit in which an act of utmost desperation had taken place. An officer had been issuing razors for shaving to inmates there, all housed in single cells. Working in corrections helps to develop certain instinct and, driven by that radar, the officer went back to check the doors of the previously served cell. Through the miniature window, he saw the inmate standing motionlessly with shoulders towards the metal doors. He had been issued his razor only moments before. The officer was about to move on but spotted a drop or two of that inmate's blood on the floor. More drops started dripping, faster ... He rushed into the cell to help. Other officers rushed there too. The desperate man had cut his own throat, aiming for the jugular. Now, he was putting up a fierce physical fight with the very people who were attempting to save his life. He was hoping to bleed out before becoming overpowered, absolutely and unequivocally wishing to die. Soon he was pinned down on the concrete floor though …

For an extremely intense moment, there was no differentiation with respect to the professional and social roles in the gloomy cell. Perhaps there were no guards and no inmate either. All present rescuers were human beings, in their powerful, synchronized improvisation, frantically scrambling to save the life of a fellow human being who so much wanted to end it. Everybody was doing what they could. Suddenly Victor found himself on his knees, right above the inmate's widely slit throat, looking like the gills of a large fish. Victor was holding a portable lamp and watching under its light the trembling hands of the nurse. She was making some progress in her valiant struggle to close, with some provisional stitches that still regularly ejected blood, widely cut throat. The fight to save a life lasted for quite some time. The situation was well in hand by the time the paramedics arrived to rush the unconscious, desperate offender to the hospital.

Afterwards, it was Victor's job to intervene with certain shaken employees, who participated in the traumatizing, bloody scene, providing support. He had to make sure that they were emotionally stabilized enough to drive home safely. The people involved talked with each other for some time, and then they drove away. For a while Victor stood alone in the empty parking lot. A brief thought, "Why has no one checked on me?" crossed his tired mind. Then the reality kicked in: "I am the prison psychologist, so I should have known better." He mutely joked to himself that he had not wasted the tax payers' money today. Soon he was driving to his empty house, where only his husky was awaiting him. All of a sudden, a black squirrel jumped on the asphalt in front of the car. It was too late to manoeuvre around it. He heard a quick, muffled noise made by his tire running over the little animal. And that was it; he was triggered …

Victor pulled over, stopping the car on the gravel shoulder of the empty country road. He was unable to drive any further. His wife had recently been killed in a motor vehicle accident and even without the events of the day, Victor was still in deep grief. The heart-wrenching fact that his marriage was "made in heaven" was not making things any easier. On the day of the accident, Victor was suddenly called out of his weekly group to the emergency room of a small local hospital. His wife brought there one hour earlier, would be in a coma soon. Helplessly looking at her disfigured face, he could still see that face's rare beauty from just that morning. She was his best friend, a full of fun and light "mother figure" for everyone around her, a very rare find.

Sitting in his car, he was fielding complex and tantalizing flashbacks—his late wife's battered and bleeding face, the inmate's opened and bleeding throat, and even that stupid squirrel flattened on the country road. All these images were blurring into one traumatic scene, modified in repetitive sequence. His normal resilience veiled by a black tsunami of desperation rolling over and over and over him. He sat paralysed, numb and, perhaps for the first time in his life, helplessly lost … Victor took several deep breaths, nevertheless, like he was trained to lead other people to do, and collected himself a little. He asked his inner voice, "What do I do now?"

As expected, that matter-of-fact, always reliable silent voice, responded with no delay, "Stop feeling sorry for yourself, it is below your integrity. Do not crawl to the corner for a pity party. Your life is much better than you think—even in this hard moment … Here, close your eyes. Do you see the darkness? Open them. What do you see? Isn't it a colourful world, with its trees, fields, and winding asphalt road? Close your eyes again. Keep them closed and intensely think that if you open them again, you will see darkness only, because you are blind … Only once you really get the message, open your eyes again, then enjoy what you see … Now, move your legs. Think hard how you would feel if you wanted to get out of your car, but could not, because you were paralysed … But you are not blind or paralysed, so you better shape up, and do it fast.

"Don't you have the two grown-up, intelligent children, building their own lives, even if far away? Are you starving in a refugee camp in the African Sahel? Are you in a war zone? Are you being tortured? Are you imprisoned for life in a solitary cell having done nothing wrong except uphold your political views? Are you leaving a doctor's office with the news that your final diagnosis is a "death sentence"? Do you feel the mighty tremor of an earthquake, or see a fast approaching, towering tidal wave?

"Even if some of these things were yours to own, would that stop the magnificent symphony of the universe, in which your essence is indestructible, one tiny note in its proper place? Moreover, you are in a beautiful and plentiful Noah's Ark of a land, where everything that exists in the world exists around you. So, enjoy your every day. You are alive and well. There are yet many things that you want to do, and even must do, in your remaining lifetime. Get up and live life or your inner voice will stop respecting you. Now just slowly and very carefully drive home to feed that husky."

Victor managed to smile faintly. His inner voice must have once read the advice of Krishna to Arjuna, offered in the Vedic text of the "Mahabharata," the ancient, epic poem of the *Bhagavad Gita*. Or, at least, must have been familiar with the pivotal Twenty-third Psalm in the *Bible*, which asserts to never be afraid, even if walking in the valley of shadows.

Victor heeded his inner voice's advice and started his car, and then drove to the village's small convenience store on his way home. He rented three movies in the "family section." He desperately felt like watching old movies, ones with messages that were clean, perhaps naive, positive, and warm. He also bought a few slices of pizza with Mediterranean toppings to take out. Victor fed his mute, blue-eyed, and furry husky, as told. Then he watched the soothingly uncomplicated stories of *Black Beauty*, *The Princess*, and *Iron Will*.

The next day he began drawing a plan for a large memorial garden that he would build with his own hands for his late wife. It would consist of a massive stone entrance, a central stone sundial, a large gazebo, and privacy fencing all around. Inside that "secret garden" there would be flower beds, decorative shrubs, as well as vegetable and herb swathes. Working on this project in his spare time, he would sweat out his grief and a degree of desperation.

Then he set about implementing his plan, building his garden, and tending it just as he planned. Over the course of several difficult years, he did in fact, grieve himself well again. Afterwards, not wanting to become just a guardian of as the past, even in a unique garden, Victor decided to move on. He sold his and his late wife's beautiful, sunny, but for too long incurably empty, pine log house, that had become a dead shell for him. The family that bought it fell in love with it at first sight.

For his part, he built a new stone-and-log small house on the shore of a shiny nearby lake, in his own "trademark" way; that is, largely with his own hands. He added a vaulted room in the attic—overlooking the calm waters of the lake and its tiny center island—appointed in pine, with the "feel" of an artist's private studio. Even though he had no use for such a room and had no idea why he was compelled to complete it—except that his inner voice told him to …

A year later, visiting Budapest, the same reliable voice unexpectedly advised him to attend a recital that somehow came to his attention. He listened to the classical music with growing pleasure. He had heard Vivaldi's healing *Four Seasons* many times in the past. This particular rendition of "Spring" transcended all others; he felt as if he was listening to … spring, alive to itself. The violinist, a stranger to him at the time, would become his future wife. That extra room in the attic—transformed to a small music studio—has become equally alive, filled with the harmonious tones of an old violin.

The Three Options

Broken, I don't know how to now carry on
After what has happened,
Shattering my trust in all
That was "supposed" to make sure
It would never happen—to me

The first and instant choice
Would be trying to fast flee from my dark pit
Through mind's pain-numbing substance
Into uncontrolled behaviour

In the second available option
I would talk to someone that I *warmly liked*
(But also *respected for a reason*)
To share my hard feelings

My third alternative
Would be to simply *calm myself regardless,*
And ask the silence in me what to do
So it whispers what it thinks

The practice seems to prove
That the *fusion* of the last two options
Will naturally bring
The golden answers at the end of the day,
Or even much sooner than that …

Part IV

Mediterranean Gardens

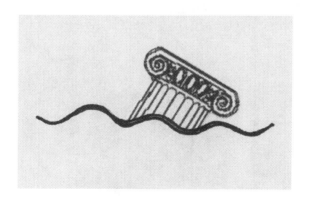

Beauty is the form under which the intellect prefers to study the world.

—Ralph Waldo Emerson

Beauty

There appears to be no clearer proof
To the existence of the Beyond,
Than the inner ability
To perceive and explore
The ever-spellbinding enigma of beauty ...

Provided one chooses to reduce
The wholeness of oneself
To transient power plays of one's body
Formed to perish—
Why such a vessel would be endowed
With the so unique
Radar seeking beauty?

All enchanting beauty seems to suggest:
Graced with joy become those
Longing to see me,
And blessed are these
Helping the others through the gifts of art
To find me,
As I am the first of all the wonders
And a magnet-beacon
Leading to silky silence ... of the Beyond

Mediterranean Legend

I am a legend of the antediluvian giants' balmy lake
An old cradle to proud civilizations ghostly passed

My body slept in shadows of their long ships' sails
In three ancient temple-colours of white, black, and red

On my southern shores the land of plenty did thrive,
Caressed by wide rivers where sand dunes glare now

To the north of my shores dwelt a deep silence of ice,
From the east side, the winds of change used to fly

Then, during most fearful day before desperate night
In the West—the coming ocean tore my walls apart

My water grudgingly turned from the sweet into salty
As I've become subjected to an ocean rule's mercy

My wave-swept islands to their former peaks shrunk
In the sea-bottom's sands I buried Titans' murky past

On my reshaped shorelines small settlers now thrive,
If next wall-waves approach some, one's soul never dies …

On the Acropolis Hill

more light …

—Johann Wolfgang Goethe

By the divine wind engulfed
Conceived as truest to self
The genius of art,
With the austere means
Of dense material expressions
Most naturally
Embarks on a mission,
In-grace creating
Its success epitomes
To be adored by many as icons

An icon acts as a lighthouse
That attracts senses,
So every faring
This no-end-sea-of-life traveler
May briefly cease
One's own
Always circling relentless pursuit,
And reflect in depth
On beauty thus truth …

By all admired manifestations
Of the proven icons,
Beyond any doubt
Offer the finest evidence
That initially fluid, even chaotic
Modest art-quests,
Could reach a grand pinnacle
In the indispensable

From any architectural icons
The one most imprinted
Into the passing us
May be the pointing
Towards more light
While standing on Earth,
Parthenon built by old wisdom

The Portrait of an Unknown Man in a Black Sariki

In this as if forgotten by the bustling shoreline
High-up-the-mountains hamlet,
(Or stony embodiment-reminder of old Crete)
A man's picture is being carefully painted
But only in the recording memory
Of his discretely "sketching" observer

The well-aged man does not realize that he poses,
Being as naturally and fully truthful
To his harmoniously pristine surroundings
As the entangled old fig tree
Under the shade of which—celebrating high noon
He simply enjoys life, and again
A miniature cup of coffee as dense as sweet tar

His silvery hair is adorned by a black *sariki* cap
One unusual, but exclusively
To the seemingly unfocused "in-memory painter,"
Surely not to the man being portrayed,
And is just obvious to his family
So too the old circle of—alike him—good friends

He wears the knee-high pitch-black *stivani* boots
Made of fine leather locally raised,
His peasant plain shirt, with the wide, loose sleeves,
Neither boasts a white collar, nor a pocket

The tall model's dignified face is manly defined
By his groomed *moustaki* in grey,
The sunken dark eyes show the power of modesty,
As he in friendly indifference glimpses
At the still memorizing him, strangely fleeting bird

Dancing on a Crater

In April—descending on Santorini fast—
One likely might feel
Like a swirling shade of a falling leaf
At the blind mercy
Of the Cycladic, high roaring winds,
Fiercely infighting
Over the island's severe beauty
Of calmly intense enormity,
While not having any escape wings
Even the mythical ones of wax

In windy April few newcomers arrive
For most would rather
Dance on the caldera in a warmer sun,
But—if and when—
One tames a pink octopus
Swimming in potatoes and onion stew
At a village basic diner's table,
One might become
Invited to a wedding party,
And still overnight dance relaxed
On the huge crater, among no-strangers

Some faint Minoan spell not withstanding
It is the natural
Not even that timeless
In such unexpected spontaneous invite,
That compels one to keep returning
To the slow fading islands
Of the best-ancient in modern Greece

On the Montenegro's Seashore

For Ton and Anjori Peters-Sengers

At dawn, by a gentle breeze evoked,
The vaguely sweet fragrance of thick pine groves
Begins to feel almost as intense,
As the crisp smell of salt, alerting the awakening shores

I stand on this tentative frontier
Dividing the patient fluidity of an infinitely supple sea
From the hard vulnerability of land,
Shown in the lacework of bays and foam-carved cliffs

Between the illusory horizon and my prone to err eyes,
Hovering above the Adriatic waves
A lone fisherman's old blue boat appears to buoy
As if suspended … in the sunlit void …

The Two Largest Peaches

So many hot summers ago,
A penniless student happy-go-lucky
On his maiden approach
Towards the calling Adriatic maze,
En route helped himself
To a sleeping-bag-freebie-night
In a mist-soaked orchard
Up in the mountains of Bosnia

At the budding red sunrise
Instead of being duly chased out
By the Muslim owner,
A trespasser was in silence offered,
Wrapped in a light smile,
The two largest peaches
From the heavy fruit basket
By that imposingly bearded man

Too many long winters passed
And "Dr. Well-To-Do"
Living in the innocently young land,
While seeing the icy plight
On a TV plasma screen
Put that man's warm, bearded face
In the frame of civil war
Much hoping—he had survived …

Dubrovnik

Craving this tangible Grail over centuries' noise past,
All the impermanent powers
Of the "Kaleidoscope Mediterraneo," forever in flux,
Have invariably opted
To swiftly encrust Dubrovnik as the unique pearl
In their by time reclaimed crowns

Is it the fabled pearl on long Croatian shores found
(As everyone seems to agree),
Or the built to be grounded,
In marble carved and with light sprinkled,
Tempting with striking beauty ark, dressed in white?

To its sun-dried peninsula dock
Endlessly touched by the azure waves' soft fingers
Come, holding hands readily,
Young pairs co-designing
The built to feel almost impersonal—new world,
In awe discovering the value
That their steely-glass milieu has refused to condone ...

That Photo from Venice '81

The by ages sculpted gondola, half-tilted,
In perpetual zeal washed
With the next waves of countless glances

It still buoys—most majestically,
Yet seems decreasingly
Docked to the foreign pier of this world …

Sunken into the heart of light dying down,
Sleep-boating—smiles
The painful beauty's ghostly-sweet finesse …

I see still embraced on a red-cloth seat
Two Venetian masks,
Alive both—deep in love with each other

An Old Village in Umbria

For Ganjifa Raghupathi Bhatta

A stone-engraved village
Tends to perch its old self
On a hill properly steep,
So it could evade
A lesser biblical flood,
A freak wave of barbarians,
Even the ever-focused
Old "good neighbourhood"

On such a suitable slope
A vineyard easily climbs,
Sheep ascend gladly
Drawn by the quality views,
Orchards nearly fly
Defying the edge of gravity
For overweight pears,
Swollen in the sun peaches

A village, limestone-defined,
Erects its opened church
At the due middle
For all gathered houses
Eclipsed by the perimeter,
Symbolizing *this way*—
The essential force
Within the walls of a body

In this self-contained village
Like a nest perched
Above the vast sunlit valleys,
Privy to the higher skies
A boy to be a painter
By the name of Raphael—
Was humbly born
Once, upon the flow of time …

The Palace on Lake Como

The terrace of this noble palace
So impeccably overlooks
The serene lake's deep sapphire,
Encrusted in a huge ring
Of the snow sparkling Alps

In this enchanted arts' studio
All of the man-made
And by nature conceived,
Have under best stars united
To exert the joint power
Over one's silenced senses,
Commanding them
To surrender into sheer beauty

It feels in chorus joyful but sad
Delving in this harmony,
As it too selectively invited
The affluent senses only
Of those privileged, so very few

Sur le Pont d'Avignon

Like strings escaping a violin's tone, dance the gentlemen dance the ladies on the bridge in Avignon ...

—Krzysztof Kamil Baczynski

Within the shadow cast in white,
Of the haunting
Half-abandoned post-papal palace,
The ancient stone bridge
Reaches out
Above seen-it-all Rhone,
Despite this empty promise
Still fails to touch
That courted ages ago
Overly distant opposite shore ...

On the slender cobblestone podium
Supported by firm arches
Erected to last,
Aging countess Melancholy
So ghostly dances
With her ageless marquis Time,
While elated
But rushing tourists
Obliviously stroll through ...

Provence-Nostra

For Bets Thomassen

Above the quaint ochre-washed "maison"
And its clay roof in Roman-red,
Beyond the olde-worlde windows
Adorned by the mistral worthy shatters
In fitting spectrum from azure to green
Complementing lavender yielding fields,
The hot sun, or flowers by Van Gogh,
Dots the chiaroscuro pointillism
With strokes of sunrise-friendly brush

It is at those cicada-rich puzzling nights
That the smart owl silently glides,
Not unlike an unidentified flying object,
It sits on the knotty tree's olive branch
Then with dry savvy by heart recites
Those scattered well, obtuse quatrains,
Scrambled by Nostradamus for a reason,
In the medieval town of nearby Salon

Terroir Grande

"*Terroir*"—is nature's long-created artwork
That absorbs its consecutive layers
Of subtly compounding
With due patience permeating themselves,
Complementing one another
Countless ingredients and influences
Forming, in their synergy,
A refined vineyard's proper prerequisite

The physical appearance of mature "*terroirs*"
Depends on the arts and crafts
Of the material world, able to blend perfectly
Its geology and botany
With rough sculptures by the local landscapes,
Fine offerings of weather,
Even the graceful minuet of heavenly bodies

Yet—old hands that structured poems in wine
Wouldn't have ever blessed
Our glasses with the ruby-red sunlight,
Infusing silk to raw fragrance,
If it was not for the ancient myth's soul
Incarnated in the Mediterranean Terroir-Grande
Which the younger world
Better never witness as passing away

The Small Farmhouse in Spain

In memory of Ernest Hemingway

A missed turn on the back roads of Castilla
May send one along too narrow dusty lanes
Through, by the vultures not forgotten hills,
To a tiny farmhouse for decades abandoned

Its plastered walls are dotted hauntingly
With densely designed irregular patterns,
Or round holes left by bullets' whistling
That put this site to death three generations ago

The worst scars may surround the open mouth
Of the door, and the two empty eyes of windows
Suggesting a hopeless, still continued fight
Until it's most plausible, unforgiving end …

Who were the soldiers shielding the lost cause,
Against stern brothers that had trapped them in?
Did their sons or daughters marry one another
In spite, pointing its future to the fading past?

The Brisk Flamenco

Announcing the inception of dawn
Here the vibrant melody of flamenco comes
On early sunbeams dancing
Faster and faster as it approaches
Unevenly accented
By rhythm of someone's clapping hands

The lone singer reveals himself to be
A short and stocky
Relaxed, aging work-bound labourer,
With the zest for life in his smiling eyes

The generous gift of food for thought
Offered free to a traveller
Who by now has well absorbed
All the charms of the slow meandering street
Leading to a mute poem in stone
Read by a few orange trees

Returning Waves

In memory of Inez de Castro y Infantado, my great-great grandmother

On a dry hill, while listening to the sublime in Alhambra's old song,
Above this historic city, one with long memory,
As a sudden lightning quickly passes
The haunting sound-scene,
Or shot by a muezzin arrow with the pike of his deep-piercing prayer
Invoking most triumphant celebrations
For young fighters with green bandanas on bowing foreheads,
Who hold in their keen hands countless
Not the ancient curved blades,
But modern assault rifles up towards the blue shield shooting,
The ecstatic rows, in wildest joy of their lives, by elders' sacrificed,
That sound and scene not existing …

It must have been the hour of too much sun
That brought this in seconds vanishing *Fata Morgana*
From a distant desert, across the Mediterranean's slow returning waves,
It just had to be an effect of too relentless heat
Or that matter-less, mysterious byte,
One unnoticeably lost by the overly busy mill of unstoppable time

Cataplana con Vinho Verde

The still life of a silvery ocean
Has rendered itself to us
As fresh *frutti de mare's*
Tastefully hot presentation
Within the round fragrant stage
Below its copper curtain
Embellished by two glasses
Of pale green wine
Reflecting a candle's pulse
Until its frail charm passes

Henry the Navigator

In this once proudly sovereign castle
Only by elements conquered
After setting the due course for his sailors,
King Henry the Navigator,
Eager to find a new route
(As being called by the eternal wind),
Surrendered all his charts and blank maps,
Leaving them with care
On an azulejo-tiled tray with the blue and yellow
Delicately fractious patterns,
Before with praise dismissing
His own faithfully serving, long shadow

The Last Window

At the very farthest due-west point
Of the tired continent,
The single last window to the West
For well-aging Europe
In this close to stormy waters
Grey stone house's wall
Overlooks the cold might of Atlantic
From an edge of the abysmal cliff
Set on the Portuguese shores

What would it be like
To live a remote life here,
Watching the swift, never-ending wind
Seen from that window's lenses?

The Joy of Life

For my daughter

Try to enjoy the great festival of life with other people.
—Epictetus

La joie de vivre … People in their fleetingly unique lives, woven into the equally unique fabric of colourful societies, have tried from times unrecorded to taste as much joy of life as is humanly possible. No wonder, as life with no joy is almost like an electrically galvanized stiff body, once used for instruction in old medical schools, one already without its warmly vibrating invisible nucleus. Such life slowly suffocates, existing, but vicariously.

There are various views from over the vanishing millennia how to distil that champagne of the soul. Most prescriptions collected in the stream of written texts have invariably retired to sleep, forgotten on silent shelves. Their primary sin, writing the merely theoretical vision, reduced them, like the winemakers' "noble rot," to the librarians' "noble dust," however enlightening.

Only the best practical prescriptions, incarnated into society's daily practice through many generations, can offer the desired outcome. When that happens, la joie de vivre—not interested or maybe even incapable of self-defining—more than gladly joins its longed-for partner, the simple, common life …

In fairness, their happy union is facilitated when blessed by certain external circumstances: azure skies, gentle warm winds, the melody of sea waves, and the fertile soil, slowly soaking in benign sunbeams. The winning, tried and true prescription for attracting the joy of life is both enticingly simple and socially resilient. It seems to climb on an ancient pillar made of white marble like a healthy ever-green grapevine …

In a garden beside an old country house with a red-tiled roof, female hands cover a long garden table with a white tablecloth and the joy of life flows in. It knows it will have a lot of fun! Not being in a hurry, it waits, watching as the white, plain tablecloth is set with the three symbols of deeper meaning. One: homemade wine, produced from one's own grapes. Two: crusty and wholesome country bread. Three: the immortal presence of aromatic, cold-pressed olive oil. *That* goes without saying, completing the ancient "Mediterranean trinity." The joy of life acknowledges these tangible symbols of rustic sanctum, masterfully created by the hard work of many skilful hands.

As the other ingredients gradually arrive on the table, deliciously sprinkled with local herbs, ephemerally adorned by the interplay of light and shade, the Mediterranean quality-time comes ... The invited guests celebrating at the long table and their guest of honour, joy of life, readily mingle. Innately multilingual, la joie de vivre is equally fluent in Greek, Hebrew, Croatian, Italian, French, Spanish, and Portuguese, without even a trace of an accent. It involves itself in lively, friendly, simultaneous conversation. It takes its time, eating with a relaxed appetite an array of antipasti from simple plates painted in harmonious colours. And it drinks plain but robust wine from thick, durable glasses.

Afterwards, the elated joy of life aptly sings, frequently motivating some local musical instruments to respond. When that happens, it is most natural for it to dance to that lively, soul-uplifting music. In some places along the unending, rugged coastline, the joy of life seems to be particularly fond of dancing in human circles. They are dynamically drawn in the early evening's air by people holding hands, or amicably putting them on their neighbours' shoulders while grinning and dancing together ...

At first gradually, then wholeheartedly, the festivities are interrupted by the delicately emerging fragrance of the expertly prepared whole lamb or goat, roasted outdoors. A good seven hours may have transpired to get that roast from bleating to table, bonding the invited guests to each other in a table of gladness. Each had taken their fifteen-minute turns at the spit, slowly revolving above the low-heat fire the equally slowly changing its colour roast, before it would be sampled and judged as ready. The relaxed rotators have at regular intervals brushed the readying roast with virgin olive oil mixed with fresh oregano. The irresistible aroma would go well with the next terracotta jar of homemade, likely red and surely hearty wine. One, placed on the long table probably by the same female hands that had put the white, plain tablecloth on it. It is with a glass of such simple, country wine, that la joie de vivre chooses to make a toast to its natural partner, which is, unsurprisingly, still the simple, common life ...

Here, in these varied lands, looked after by the unfathomably antique, reminiscent of a classic golden medallion Mediterranean sun, the joy of life remains dormant only, while the guns thunder and the soldiers march, singing their fiercely proud, then helplessly sombre songs. However, as long as people can remember, la joie de vivre has always invincibly woken up afterwards, to naturally enjoy itself once again.

The mysterious but resilient, sublime yet simple joy of life, may be sipping this longevity-champagne from the forgotten chalice of the prerecorded past. Perhaps, the mythological vines for that liquid, infused with light, once upon a time were planted, carefully and lovingly, under differently aligned constellations. Planted under the endlessly patient supervision of the unhurriedly traversing configurations of the same stars that look the same everywhere on this still young blue garden Earth, just from slightly different perspectives ...

Atlantis

For what secret reason this depth-sunken ghost of a city
Ever fell down for the planet Earth,
Fleeing the native constellations of the parental skies?

How a curious octopus feels about this cryptic demise
Exploring with its soft waving arms a collapsed pillar
Of an enormous colonnade,
What it realizes not
When the dim sunlight touches the rubble of a roof?

Why this motionless pentagram, or a crimson starfish
Has opted to mark the submerged middle
In the concentric circles built of the stones, set to stars?

And for how long this black flame, or a sea snake,
Has been enlightening
A doomed wall's wide crack, half-buried in white sand?
May that snake hear those love words once said
Under, back then, the sweetest fig tree in that city lost?

What faith adhere to the swift members
Of this colourful fast-moving, but mute congregation,
Ready to flow in through the crushed portal of gloom?

Whom do they yearn to worship in that temple in which,
After the subtlest deliberations of sages with high priests,
All agreed upon the Definition:
IT—is the Absolute of Being-Happiness-Consciousness?

Is it that yard where he saw her gently firm lips' outline
As she sensed his eyes' gift of sincerity,
In the singular atom of time that has remained intact here?

A Hermit

For Jerzy Bahr

Until his quiet passage
Into unknown,
He in silence resolved
To delve in seclusion,
And exist fully devoid
Of all others,
So they would not be able
To continue erecting
Their living wall
Between him and the unknown
Anymore

Why hasn't he remained
Amongst us,
Building in his lone heart
The stairs towards that unknown,
In silence made
Of our hollow sorrows
And brief joys?

Via Illuminativa

The lifelong way to illumination—steeping towards end
Starts as a multitude of unchartered paths,
With the proverbial movement of the first, shy step and
That baseline yet poignant question:
Is there anything more than what can be touched or seen?

If that seemingly impractical question
Is truly posed, thus permeating one's mind enough deeply,
Some half-answers begin crossing
The semi-permeable border
Between mundane and meagre realism
And a broader outlook bound to sublime it

Then at the pivotal point it occurs
On this solitary winding and hard way—
A new feeling of fearless calm joyfully begins pouring in
Through a slowly opening dam
Between heart and mind—gradually enlightening the path

Illumination, naturally evolves along its lucid continuum,
Where the innately sprouting light
Offers the state in which a soul, compelled to travel early,
Sooner sees or touches the essence
Of oneself, the others, the way—but never the destination—
As it chooses to stay incredibly far away
While remaining much closer … unimaginably close …

Having fulfilled itself, during its lives-exhausting journey,
After the endless exposures to time and space,
Fully completed illumination now fuses with its destination
Submerging in it, with *most trusting love* …

The Prayer of the Garden

In memory of Pierre Teilhard de Chardin

We have always avoided defining ourselves as a *Process*
Or even as a garden—one tended by someone …
We simply wish to just breathe,
Sip the generosity of the clear liquid allowing us to exist,
Digest the wealth of organic nutrients,
Bask in the sun riches during our summer heydays,
Be blessed by rain in spring and fall,
And in the fertile womb of long winter, dream healingly
Surely bound to come back
As we do not know better than clinging to our old selves
Whether the fragrantly refined flowers,
The common weeds, those most resilient plants,
Rare and inherently different—poison brewing bushes,
Or by far the majority of the waving us …
We all wish only to last, stretching our asking arms
Towards this burning out star
Whether we turn hollow, therefore leafless,
Or sprout the newest, hence light-friendly, yielding buds …
If we are a garden—do we have gardeners?
We do not think so—unless they silently come at night
And do the inexplicable work while we sleep
The one we cannot for a reason see …
Yet—why had it forever been
That at dark times we do feel bent, burnt, cut, and halved
After reciprocally invading our habitats
But at bright periods become nourished well
Regenerated and realigned, for starting all—fresh again?
Is it just we—or the gardeners—or both
Or is it even much more than that?
Then again—if we have gardeners it could suggest to us
That our potential has been of importance
To the powers unimaginable
As tending to us would command such a triad
Of depth-might-longevity we as yet *could not relate to* …
We pray that time moulding us harshly

Will indeed become shortened …
We pray for our gardeners—if they exist—to love us all
Irrespective of how far we stray
From their lofty dreams, their ironclad plans …
We pray to touch once some of the lands unseen
We now pray that the real meaning of our lives will soon
Be with loving wisdom revealed to us,
So we could turn the first page in one of the oldest books

The Prayer of the Gardeners

or The Code of Cosmic Gardeners ...

Sages describe us as guardians—or even as angels,
But we have preferred, despite this,
To think of ourselves to be as *very old gardeners*

We've not designed this peripheral garden-in-blue,
One in an endlessly dispersed chain,
We have been sent here only to assure its growth

We toil long—trying to follow the grand design
On behalf of the unknown designer
Who, from a touch indirect, has bestowed his plan ...

Even though our powers to implement the future
May appear to be limitless,
This is only from the viewpoint of the garden itself

We pray for wisdom in deciphering that set design,
Enacting it on the material plane,
And minimizing our errors, too difficult to avoid ...

We pray for being able to protect this round garden
From an outer impact voiding its harvest,
And for correlating the small blows, with gardening

Also for prudence—by pruning the feeble branches,
Cutting off the rotten stems
To replace all depleted or dead-old, with new growth

We pray for love—while tending to that newest
In our gliding, blue garden,
To all—what promises our sought-after *value-yield* ...

We are the aging gardeners, who begin to feel tired
After tending this sleeping garden
Over the millennia lost, profoundly forgotten by it

We pray—once our thorny task becomes completed—
The unknown designer will allow us
To forget it all in the *joy-garden* he designed as his …

The Silence of the Unknown Designer

In memory of John Paul II

Love is an affinity which links and draws together the elements of the world …
love, in fact, is the agent of universal synthesis.

—Pierre Teilhard de Chardin

I may also be:
My own *joyful silence*, imbued in motion,
One self-designing to become filled
With any sounds it pleases to conceive,
Which all, during the formative periods,
Delve in the original sin of pure illusion—
Of living separate from my oldest silence,
Into which those sounds gradually must return
Over the eon-seconds, spiralling
In what is perceived as the flow of time

I micromanaged creation principally once
When in the absolute of my still memory
I've drawn my blueprint, turned into motion
Empowered with my living energies …
Now in sheer patience, gently bottomless,
I wait—for the pre-designed in detail results,
While my endlessly optional blueprint
Layer after layer learns to read … itself

The fading, then renewing mega-galaxies
Are mere cells within my denser apparition …
The worlds of entities spiritually aging
Labour as the old-hand gardener-protectors
Of the new ones leaning towards the light
To come of age, and serve me the same way,
For after dissolving their fears they find
That I am truth and seek love from them …

I await them, as they at the slow pace grow,
Could read a fraction of my own memory,
Feel responsible for that atom of my design,
Therefore from their trials marked by errors
Could become a miniscule, yet active part
Of my set motion—beyond anyone's fathom,
With the aim, increasingly dearer to them,
To help *all sailing sparks of my vested love*
In coming back, to the *joyful silence of mine* …

About this Book

Witold Poplawski's intriguing, independently formed literary work both interweaves and interlocks prose with poetry in an innovative and rewardingly accessible way. *Blue Garden* artistically explores, with lucid realism, as well as wit, the moral and spiritual dimension in common human existence. This thought-provoking volume is offered by a psychologist and writer to any reader who formulates questions about their place and direction within the overwhelming complexity of our turbulent, rapidly changing world.

Blue Garden is also a charitable project in book form. The author's proceeds will go to the charity that assists children in most dire of needs. (See the author's note in the front section.)

About the Author

Witold Poplawski, PhD, once a coal miner, factory worker, and university lecturer, is a psychologist in Ontario. An award-winning author, he has been honoured with a Decoration of Merit to Polish Culture, a Minister's Award for Exceptional Humanitarian Service from the Government of Ontario, and an Award for Commitment to Volunteerism from the Ontario Premier. His works are accomplished in a second language, acquired later in life. He lives on a lake in a small log and stone house, built largely with his own hands. His passion/hobby is manual labour, particularly stone masonry and gardening.